OVERDUE AND
PRESUMED LOST

OVERDUE AND ★
★ PRESUMED LOST
The Story of the USS Bullhead

By MARTIN SHERIDAN

BLUEJACKET BOOKS

Naval Institute Press
Annapolis, Maryland

Naval Institute Press
291 Wood Road
Annapolis, MD 21402

© 1947 by Martin Sheridan

First Bluejacket Books printing, 2004

Library of Congress Cataloging-in-Publication Data
Sheridan, Martin, 1914–
        Overdue and presumed lost : the story of the U.S.S.
Bullhead / by Martin Sheridan.
        p. cm. – (Bluejacket books)
        Originally published: Francestown, N.H.: M. Jones, 1947.
        ISBN 1-59114-786-7 (alk. paper)
        1. Bullhead (Submarine) 2. World War, 1939–1945–
Naval operations–Submarine. 3. World War, 1939–1945–Naval
operations, American. 4. World War, 1939–1945–Campaigns–
Pacific Area. I. Title. II. Series.
        D783.5.B8S5 2004
        940.54'51–dc22
                                                    2003061510

Printed in the United States of America on acid-free paper ∞
11 10 09 08 07 06 05 04   9 8 7 6 5 4 3 2 1

DEDICATION

THIS book is dedicated primarily to the 84 gallant Americans who sailed from Fremantle, Australia, on July 31, 1945, on the third and final war patrol of the USS BULLHEAD, the last ship lost to enemy action during the war. She is now classified in United States Navy archives as "overdue and presumed lost."

That phrase offers an indomitable challenge to anyone's imagination, yet the fate of a large percentage of the submarines lost in World War II remains an insoluble mystery — now and forever — since few underwater craft have ever had any survivors. Submarines were, indeed, the silent service.

Fifty-two American submarines were lost during the war from enemy action, mechanical failure, or accident. The Navy has announced 43 of the total as "overdue from war patrol and presumed lost." What has happened to most of these craft and their crews is Davy Jones' profound secret.

It was the author's privilege during the war to be the only War Correspondent allowed to accompany a submarine on active war patrol. He offers "Overdue and Presumed Lost" as a tribute to the USS BULLHEAD, officially considered to be the best trained submarine in the Force, and to the 42 other missing submersibles.

PREFACE

UPON graduation from Submarine School in 1936, the officer in charge told us that to be a good submariner one must be not only easy to live with but also pleasant to live with.

When we arrived at Guam before taking off into enemy-controlled waters and I was informed of the fact that I was to take along a war correspondent, I mentally threw up my hands; but we found "Scoop" Sheridan both pleasant and easy to live with. He was a fine shipmate whom we were glad to have aboard.

It is unfortunate that when a correspondent was finally permitted to make a war patrol, there were so few enemy ships left to sink. However, our patrol was an interesting one, and I'm sure that "Scoop" was just as happy that there were no more bombs and depth charges than there were (so were we all).

I had the honor to command the USS BULLHEAD during her first two war patrols and was transferred to the Operations Staff of the Commander, Submarine Force, Pacific Fleet, only a month before the submarine and my shipmates were lost. However, I am certain the men of the BULLHEAD met their death courageously in the highest traditions of the United States Navy.

This book will impress everyone interested in submarines, especially the next of kin of the men aboard the SS-332, for it presents in great detail the war accomplishments of the BULLHEAD.

WALTER T. GRIFFITH,
Commander, USN

Newport, R. I.

CONTENTS

LIST OF ILLUSTRATIONS

FOREWORD

The author desires to thank and acknowledge the help of:

The Navy Department for making this great adventure possible and providing many of the photographs.

Comdr. Walter T. Griffith, USN, who was so cooperative during the BULLHEAD'S first patrol and spent considerable time going over the details of his second patrol.

Lieut. John P. Doherty, USN, James J. Brantley, and Mrs. Edward R. Holt, Jr., for filling in facts that helped to make this the complete story of the BULLHEAD.

Win Brooks for permission to include his stirring poem, "Message From Submarine Overdue," first published in The Saturday Evening Post.

The Electric Boat Company for making available the color plates for the jacket illustration and furnishing other illustrations.

Victor Johnson for selecting and scaling down the photographs and drawing the end papers.

* * * * *

I have always been deeply interested in submarines and submariners, especially after my visit to the Submarine School at New London, just before the United States became a fighting participant in World War II. While obtaining material for magazine and newspaper feature stories and shooting photographs, I went out for several practice dives aboard one of the old R-boats used for training new crews in Long Island Sound.

I visited the late Simon Lake several times in Milford, Conn., and New York City, and took up the cudgels in his campaign for the construction of cargo-carrying submarines to sneak supplies to our Allies in Europe. German U-boats were then sinking our merchant ships faster than we could replace them. Later, after war had been declared, I returned to the Submarine Base for additional data and made several dives in a 25 year old O-boat.

When I first went to the Pacific as a war correspondent, I inquired about my chances of going on a submarine war patrol but the answer was "No." Scores of other writers had requested this permission also and all had been denied it.

Upon returning to Guam, March 10, 1945, from the first devastating low level B-29 fire-bombing of Tokyo, I had participated in just about all the different operations of war. I asked Rear Admiral H. B. "Min" Miller, Fleet Admiral Nimitz's public information officer, if I could go out on a submarine war patrol to climax my Pacific assignment.

"I can't see why not," he replied. "I'll take it up at the Admiral's conference this morning."

Twenty minutes later, he returned and asked me, "When do you want to leave?"

I needed about three days to write several yarns remaining in my notebooks and to clean up personal affairs. Miller told me to advise him when I was ready. Then he introduced me to Admiral Lockwood, who arranged to pick me up with my sea bag at CinCPac (Admiral Nimitz's headquarters) after the regular conference March 21.

To my office I sent a brief note announcing I would be unable to contact them for several weeks. In addition, I prepared several letters, each dated two weeks apart, and left them with Lieut. Comdr. Joseph Mutrie, the Coast Guard's public information officer in the Pacific, to be mailed at the proper intervals to Mrs. Sheridan so she would not feel neglected.

Thus prepared, I met Vice Admiral Lockwood in

his jeep and drove to the fleet landing where we boarded his launch for the ride to his flagship anchored in Apra Harbor. Aboard ship, Admiral Lockwood chatted with me about his submarine force for a half hour.

"Submarines continue to amaze me," said the top admiral of one of the most efficient organizations in the Navy. "There is no limit to what they can do. I sincerely wish I could go with you, you lucky fellow. My own requests to go out on war patrol have been turned down several times. Reckon the boss (Nimitz) thinks I'm too old."

Pleasant, quiet spoken and blue eyed, his brown hair belied his 55 years. Only a few gray hairs were visible at his temples. A few months later, however, the tremendous responsibility of Lockwood's command began to leave its visual impression on him.

"I joined the Navy to see the world," he explained, "but I got only as far as the Philippines before submarines got me. I've been in them ever since."

I was shown the complicated communications setup aboard the flagship and was taken into the secret operations office. There, I saw the huge wall map where scores of magnetic markers bearing the names of our submarines showed their approximate positions throughout the Pacific. My eyes popped and my mouth must have hung open, when I read some of the places where American submarines were patrolling that day.

Unlike most top-ranking officers, Admiral Lockwood rarely dined alone. At lunch, he had three submarine skippers, (rotund Comdr. Hiram Cassedy, Comdr. Robert Sellars and Comdr. Walter T. Griffith), Capt. Richard G. Voge, his operations officer, and several other men as guests.

Admiral Lockwood introduced me to Comdr. Griffith as "the war correspondent who's going along with you. The sky's the limit, Griff. Don't withhold anything except top secret and ultra information."

After lunch, Lockwood decorated the three submariners for accomplishments on previous patrols and the party retired to the briefing room while I pounded out my last dispatch to the Boston Globe. An hour later, I handed the story to Admiral Lockwood who promised to drop it off at the Press office. He gripped my hand and wished us good hunting and Godspeed.

MARTIN SHERIDAN

Watertown, Mass.

INTRODUCTION

IT WAS with considerable surprise one sunny day in March 1945, that I received Martin Sheridan aboard my flagship in Apra Harbor, Guam, and learned from him that he had permission from proper authority to make a war patrol in a submarine of my Force.

I knew that many requests had been made for permission to make war patrols but, thus far, none had been granted. This indicated a change in policy which I welcomed, since letters, usually from parents of lads in submarines, frequently asked for news of the accomplishments of their sons and propounded the question, "Is the Submarine Force the silent service or are submariners merely the forgotten men?"

Of course, they did not realize just how publicity regarding submarine operations would seriously endanger the lives of their sons, and of many other mothers' sons, by informing the enemy where submarines hunted, how they detected their targets, how they made their kills, and how they escaped the vengeance of enemy anti-submarine vessels. These, and many other data like them, our own anti-submarine forces would have given a great deal to learn about Japanese submarines, in order to more easily hunt them down and destroy them with the deadly depth charge or with an even deadlier torpedo fired from a waiting submarine.

However, for a non-technical man, a civilian interested only in human interest angles, in newsworthy happenings in the daily life of submariners, to make a war patrol — that could do much good and no harm at all.

Therefore, I welcomed Martin Sheridan as the man whose writing could answer the questions of many anxious mothers, wives and sweethearts. I gave him our own censorship rules, introduced him to his future skipper, Comdr. Walter T. Griffith, USN, one of our most outstanding and successful submariners, and wished him "Good luck and good hunting."

I have read with much interest and pleasure, in newspaper serial form, the articles of Martin Sheridan written during the first war patrol of the USS BULL-HEAD, one of our latest standard type submarines. Here he has compiled the complete story of the BULL-HEAD, from the day she was launched in Groton, Conn., to that ill-fated day in the final weeks of the war when she disappeared in the Java Sea.

He has written a most interesting account, true to life, and has very quickly absorbed the "esprit de corps" and the fine tradition of the submarine just as he has accurately divined the quiet, intent, purposeful spirit that dwells within her people. The submarine was a deadly engine of war to her crew; every day on patrol the war was at their doorstep — and the game wasn't being played for marbles. Such is the spirit Sheridan paints with words into his picture of submarine men.

His work is thorough and so well done as to interest even veteran submarine sailors. We wonder how he found out so much so quickly. That secret, no doubt, lies in his keen powers of observation and in his ready understanding of men.

I wish "Overdue and Presumed Lost" great success and I hope its author will often take up his pen to give the American public glimpses into the lives of the splendid men and ships which I have had the honor to command. Submarines will find a berth for him any time.

VICE ADMIRAL CHARLES A. LOCKWOOD, JR., USN
(*Former Commander, Submarine Force, Pacific Fleet*)
Washington, D. C.

OVERDUE AND
PRESUMED LOST

FIRST WAR PATROL

1

THIS is the story of men who go down to and UNDER the sea in ships. Audacious, defiant, and stubbornly aggressive men — all volunteers — who have served on the far-ranging underseas craft of the United States Navy's Submarine Service. Men whose courage is as deep as the enemy waters they have patrolled, and as enduring as the enviable records they have established since that memorable day in December 1941, when the Japanese loosed their aerial bombs on Pearl Harbor and plunged this country into a Pacific War of such vast proportions as to be without equal in history.

With slightly more than one per cent of the Navy's total personnel, the comparatively tiny Submarine Service achieved the destruction of so large a portion of Japanese steel merchant shipping and warships* (4,871,-600 tons) and damaged so many other vessels as to have sped the end of our island-hopping warfare by several months. It was highly perilous work, and the percentage of lives lost was higher than in any other branch of the armed forces: 16 per cent of the officers, 13 per cent of the enlisted men who actually served in submarines.

Immediately after the Japanese attacks on Pearl Harbor and Manila, our fleet submarines, the only warships able to operate independently of a large task force, be-

---

*Allied submarines sank 1,750 Japanese merchant vessels (over 100 tons), 194 combat vessels and countless smaller craft.

cause of their ability to submerge and surprise the enemy, began to prowl the blue Pacific in pitifully small numbers in search of targets for their lethal torpedoes and deck guns. Those were desperate days.

Although these submarines were operating deep in enemy waters entirely on their own, they tackled anything and everything that came their way. Neither size nor numbers mattered one whit. Submarine commanders picked on the big fellows as well as the small: they also tore into groups of five and six. Said one skipper, "The bigger they come, the better the target, and the faster they sink."

American submarines evacuated military personnel and civilians from the Philippines and delivered food and equipment to hardy guerillas remaining in the islands. They poked fearlessly into Tokyo Bay. In ever increasing numbers, they conducted unrestricted warfare and wolf-packed Japanese merchantmen and tankers in the Netherlands East Indies, off the French Indo-China coast, off China, Formosa, the Japanese main islands, and among hundreds of Pacific islands and atolls from the Solomons to the Aleutians.

Time and again, these submarines severed Japanese lines of communication with captured islands. They conducted invaluable photographic reconnaissance of enemy beaches weeks prior to the arrival of our invasion troops. They laid mines in shallow water. They thoroughly demoralized enemy supply lines with their war of attrition, sent jammed enemy troopships to the bottom and established a highly efficient lifeguard service that saved the lives of 504 men from American planes shot down within sight of Japan itself and elsewhere in unfriendly territory in the Pacific.

Our submarines tore into the once highly-vaunted Japanese Imperial Navy and tightened a strangling tourniquet around the far-flung Japanese lifelines until only a trickle of indispensable oil, tin, zinc, rice, rubber, quinine, gold, nickel, and other stolen natural resources was able to reach the Empire.

Up to September 3, 1943, the Jap Navy had lost one third of its available tonnage, with American submarines credited with the destruction of 77 per cent of that lost fleet.

Several new submersibles were joining our Pacific Fleet each month. Many were under construction at the Portsmouth (N. H.) and Mare Island (Calif.) Navy Yards; at the Electric Boat Company's yards at Groton, Conn., at the Manitowoc Shipbuilding Company's yards at Manitowoc, Wis., and at the Cramp Shipbuilding Company, Camden, N. J.

The keel for submarine 332 (later named the USS Bullhead) was laid on October 21, 1943, at the Victory Yard of the Electric Boat Company in Groton. There, amid the deafening cacaphony created by thousands of workmen working with chipping and sledge hammers, rivet guns, trucks, yard locomotives, and overhead cranes, the new submarine began to take shape. Through the winter months, they labored to speed the craft to completion.

The following spring, a lean, battle-weary submarine skipper reported to the Commander of the Submarine Base at New London for duty as an instructor at the Prospective Commanding Officers' School. He was Lieut. Comdr. Walter T. Griffith, fresh in from Fremantle, Australia, after completing four highly successful and gruelling war patrols as commanding officer of the USS Bowfin. On his first run, he had destroyed 70,948 tons of Japanese shipping, a record that stood for over two years.

Shore duty in those days did not harmonize with Griffith's highly nervous disposition, and he soon put in a request for sea duty. Submarines were being launched more rapidly than new submarine officers were graduating, so the Navy quickly assigned the carrot-topped Louisianian to command the new Bull-head, under construction only a few miles down the river.

At 7 p.m. on July 16, 1944, the submarine was scheduled to be launched, the 57th underseas craft to be built by the Electric Boat Company after Pearl Harbor. Her sponsor was Mrs. Grace Moody Doyle of Groton, wife of a yard employee who won the privilege of naming the sponsor in an election held under a special Navy directive.

Shortly before the appointed hour, the blue sky turned angry gray and broke into a heavy summer thunderstorm. Strong gusts of wind drove sheets of blinding rain into the faces of the crew and the few invited civilian guests, among whom was a full blooded Indian. The heavens reverberated with sharp claps of thunder: everyone was drenched to the skin. By 7:15, the sudden blow had cleared sufficiently to permit the launching of the Bullhead, which had withstood the rain far better than the guests' clothes.

"Guess we ought to have smooth sailing from here on," remarked Comdr. Griffith to his executive officer, dark haired Lieut. Keith R. Phillips. "This storm should be a good omen."

The craft slid almost unnoticed into the Thames River and rolled unsteadily for a few seconds like a new-born calf until she gained her sea legs. At that very moment, sections of another keel were being lowered into place on the same ways for a new submarine.

Comdr. Griffith then moved the Bullhead to an Electric Boat Company fitting out pier and began to round up his full crew. As a nucleus, he used three capable enlisted men who had served with him through four war patrols on the Bowfin and had asked to go along on the Bullhead. The trio included electrician's mate 1st class, Joseph W. Jones, of Rule, Texas; torpedoman 3rd class, Jack P. Markham, of Hornell, N. Y., and torpedo-man 1st class, William E. Short, of Jackson Heights, N. Y., already veterans of 9, 10, and 11 war patrols, respectively. In addition, the skipper chose for his engineering officer, Lieut. John P. (Pat) Doherty, USN, who had held the same assignment under him for three patrols on the Bowfin.

Other men were assigned to the Bullhead. Griffith was made a full commander in September, and by December 4, 1944, the submarine's commissioning date, he had his full complement of 85 officers and enlisted men aboard. Five officers (including the skipper) and 26 enlisted men had completed excursions into enemy waters, but the remaining 54 men were recent graduates from the Submarine School.

At the commissioning, the Navy announced a change of policy by revealing the name of the vessel and the names of the captain and other principal officers for the first time since the war began. Heretofore, officers had been identified with submarines only after they had completed their tour of duty, and submarines remained nonentities until they had engineered some spectacular accomplishments or were lost.

A crew of civilians moved the Bullhead to her pier at the Submarine Base at 1:50 p.m. on December 4, and the formal commissioning ceremony began shortly thereafter with the mustering of the ship's company top-side in blues.

Capt. H. H. McLean, then commanding officer of the Base, read the Navy Department's authorization for acceptance of the Bullhead. He was followed by Capt. W. W. Foster, representing the Electric Boat Co., who formally presented the submarine to the Navy.

"I accept the Bullhead for the United States Navy from the Electric Boat Company," said Capt. McLean.

At this point the Submarine Base band began to play the national anthem. Crewmen on the boat then performed their first official duty by breaking out the colors, union jack, and commissioning pennant from their respective masts.

Holding several sheets of white paper with hands that shook slightly, Comdr. Griffith read his orders from the Navy Department in Washington, assigning him to command the vessel. The brief ceremonies were concluded with a prayer by Chaplain H. F. Murphy.

Before dismissing the crew, however, Griffith called Jones, Markham, and Short forward and presented them Presidential Unit Citation ribbons commemorating the second outstanding war patrol of the Bowfin in November 1943, commanded by him at that time.

With 54 green men aboard, Comdr. Griffith had to conduct a fast and furious intensive training program, to whip everyone into shape as a smooth-working team for warfare against Jap shipping in the Pacific. The Bullhead had a month's shakedown training in Narragansett Bay before sailing early in January for two weeks' additional training off Key West. It was primarily diving practice, because a submarine's chief stock in trade is a speedy dive. Also on the agenda were many gunnery sessions and maneuvers with destroyers and smaller craft to perfect the use of radar and sound gear.

Next stop for the Bullhead was the Canal Zone. More training and maneuvers and lively liberty parties in gay night spots ashore.

"We're about ready, men," Comdr. Griffith announced one day. "Have your fun here, and get all the playfulness out of your system, because from now on there's going to be hard work and plenty of it."

In February 1945, the Bullhead cleared Balboa and departed for Pearl Harbor and points beyond. On the first day out, the new submarine experienced a close call that might have led to a repetition of the "Squalus" disaster had it not been for quick thinking by the skipper.

FIRST WAR PATROL

During a routine practice dive, the main induction valve failed to close fast enough because the hydraulic pressure was low. Tons of water flooded the big valve before it could be shut, but Griffith compensated for this by shifting ballast and pumping out water and continuing the dive. The incident sobered the new men to the realization that complete knowledge of their post was essential for their own safety and for the safety of everyone aboard.

The Bullhead arrived without further incident at Pearl Harbor, where Griffith picked up the latest charts and directives, and his commissary officer, Lieut. (jg) Raymond W. Strassle, USN, rustled up fresh meat, fruit, vegetables, and canned goods till the refrigerators and food lockers were packed tight. Everyone had a brief liberty ashore in teeming Honolulu, and sent home the usual souvenir — a cellophane skirt.

Following the nine day stopover, the new sub picked her way through the tortuous channels of Pearl Harbor and left the Hawaiian Islands for an uneventful trip to Guam. There, she tied up alongside the submarine tender, Holland, where Vice Admiral Charles A. Lockwood, Jr., Commander, Submarine Force, Pacific Fleet, had established his advance base headquarters.

2

March 21 — Only the metallic clanging of a ranting dredge, and the incessant lapping of water against the Bullhead's hull disturbed the tranquility and relaxation of the warm afternoon. The sun beat down fiercely, and some of the men had slipped out of their scivvy shirts to enjoy a sun bath on the slatted deck of the submarine. Others, preoccupied with the anticipation of their first war patrol, just stood around and spoke softly.

Below in the tiny wardroom, officers had finished reading and sealing the last letters the crew would be able to send their families for several weeks. They were the usual uninformative letters composed by submariners operating under the strictest censorship.

"Don't worry, darling . . . . You won't be hearing from me for a while . . . . But keep on writing . . . every day . . . . Your letters mean so much to me . . . . "

The censors' job was a comparatively simple one, since the men knew exactly what they were not permitted to write and they proceeded not to write it. That kept deletions with a razor blade at a minimum. The mail orderly stood by patiently until the censors stamped the last envelopes with *"Passed by Naval Censor"* and initialed them. Then he stuffed the mountain of letters into his brown leather pouch, climbed topside, hurried across a narrow gangway to the submarine alongside, and went up another gangway to the dark gray tender.

A moment later, the old man hurried aboard and everyone instinctively straightened up to attention. Comdr. Walter T. Griffith and the other skippers of our wolf pack* had just been briefed. Our skipper had been decorated with a Gold Star Medal in lieu of a second Navy Cross for his last successful war patrol on the Bowfin.

From under a khaki scrambled egg cap, his pale eyes squinted at the exec's wrist watch.

"We're getting underway at three, Keith," said Griffith. "Let's start the engines. And here's a passenger for us. MISTER Sheridan meet Lieut. Phillips, my executive officer."

Then an aside to Phillips, "Sheridan is a CIVILIAN war correspondent!"

Phillips was flabbergasted, I know, and his eyes blinked in amazement. But he recovered rapidly, and turned on his heel to pass the word for getting underway to the engineering officer, Pat Doherty. Clouds of pale gray smoke soon belched from the exhaust at the stern as the 16-cylinder Diesels turned over.

Back came the mail orderly, and the men began to disappear down hatches. It was exactly three o'clock when the gangway was taken in and the skipper sang out, "Take in four. Take in one. All back full."

The engines throbbed powerfully below deck, and the black-hulled, low-silhouetted sub began to slide back slowly from a sister ship, barely avoiding a large mooring buoy as she swung around.

"Ahead one third, left full rudder," ordered the captain.

The harbor water churned madly at the stern when the twin screws were reversed. The boat shuddered to a halt, then moved forward slowly as the screws took hold. We passed LST's, Liberty ships, transports, and assorted small craft in the harbor.

---

*Comdr. Hiram Cassedy, the pack leader, had the Tigrone. Also with us was Comdr. Bob Sellars (classmate of Griffith's) on the Blackfish. The Seahorse was with the group for the first few days, then changed course for a special assignment. Her skipper, Comdr. Harry Greer, had been executive officer on the old R-boat I was aboard in New London.

OVERDUE AND PRESUMED LOST

The USS Bullhead, newest submarine to join the Pacific Fleet, was only beginning her first war patrol but she had already lost that gleaming appearance of newness. Seaweed was adhering to her once shiny black hull and large patches needed painting.

Men were busy all over the place. Some were stowing away lines below the superstructure; others had disassembled the small deck guns and slipped them into their watertight compartments. They slammed tight all the deck hatches except the one in the conning tower.

In a moment, the sub began to roll gently as she neared the mouth of Apra Harbor. Atop a rusty, jaggedly perpendicular cliff, a small signal tower flashed us, "Good luck." After clearing the submarine net, our boat nosed into the long, deep swells and took green water over the bow.

Another submersible, just returning from a patrol, passed us at 300 yards; the lookouts on both bridges waved greetings. Soon, the cinnamon coastline of Guam disappeared in the thick film of tropical haze and spray, rising from the angry water pounding relentlessly against unyielding rock. Great masses of white clouds towered above the island, just as they did above every island in the Pacific. A heavy rain squall hit us at 4:30, and speedily cleared the bridge of everyone not on watch.

In the wardroom below, I met the rest of the officers. There was Lieut. Earl D. Hackman, Jr., USN, torpedo and gunnery officer, making his first patrol. The aide to the exec was Lieut. (jg) Eldridge A. Erickson, USNR, whom I soon nicknamed the "Gloomy Dane," because of his dour disposition. The others were: Lieut. (jg) Paul A. Gossett, USN, Lieut. (jg) Raymond W. Strassle, USN, Lieut. (jg) Donald Henriksen, communications officer, and Ens. Jack Simms II, USNR, assistant communicator and sound officer, who was called Junior.

They found a few small empty drawers and some locker space for my belongings. I took possession of the only remaining bunk, the one below Jack Simms', against the outboard bulkhead in the wardroom.

At sundown the boat was rigged for red. This meant that all the white lights below deck were extinguished and gloomy red ones substituted, thus enabling the crew to go on watch or to battle stations without dark-adapting their eyes before climbing on deck.

The submarine was rolling badly when I hit the sack at 7:45. It was an uncomfortable night for all and many new men were seasick. The next morning, their faces were the color of pistachio ice cream; some were unable to stand watch. I didn't have mal de mer, but I was exhausted from the night long struggle to prevent myself from falling out of my bunk.

March 22 — The sea continued to jolt us like a bucking bronco while we slithered along toward our patrol area. Griffith ordered a routine trim dive to 100 feet where the ship remained motionless. I decided this was the place to ride out heavy weather. The skipper said we were heading for the southern tip of Formosa to stand lifeguard duty for aviators on air strikes in support of the Okinawa campaign.

March 23 — Our liquid road smoothed out a bit. So did the sick men's frowns. I went topside for the first time in 48 hours and was surprised at how invigorating the fresh air smelled. Just like walking into a cold storage room.

At midnight, we established radar contact with more than a dozen warships. They were soon identified as friendly, and we decided they were part of the great task force about to invade Okinawa. We politely changed our course to get out of their way. They, too, changed course at the same time and two destroyers suddenly began to close in on us at 20 knots. This was the sort of thing that aged submariners prematurely.

We finally had to zig 15 miles off our course to avoid the fleet.

"God, I wish we were in the China Sea," growled the skipper. "Then all we'd have to worry about would be the Japs. Sometimes our own ships and planes give us more damned trouble than the enemy. Only last night a B-29 dropped a few sticks of bombs near the Seahorse, who was minding her own business in a safety lane*. Then the zoomies strafed her with machine guns but they missed."

March 24 — The Bullhead encountered more friendly ships and planes. Guessed we were sending a mammoth fleet for the upcoming attack. (The Navy said 1,500 ships were in the naval force.) By mid afternoon, the sea again became choppy and our submarine tossed around once more like the proverbial eggshell. The round hull made her a natural for easy rolling.

Sunday, March 25 — Weather: overcast and rainy. After a filling chicken dinner and ice cream, I climbed up the conning tower ladder to the bridge for my constitutional. Took only three breaths of fresh air as I didn't want to overdo a good thing. The rain served as a reminder to the captain, for he decreed this as bath day, with showers permitted all hands.

We passed between Luzon and Formosa this afternoon and entered enemy waters for the first time. Suddenly a twin engine Jap bomber popped out very low from behind clouds only four miles away. That's much too close for comfort.

"Clear the bridge!" yelled the OD.

I slid down the ladder to the conning tower, while the Klaxon was sounding twice. From the squawk box rattled the words, "Dive the boat! Dive the boat!"

---

*The Submarine Service established certain zones and lanes to be followed by submarines en route to and from their patrol areas. Our planes were instructed NOT to molest ANY submarines found in these safety lanes.

On my heels came the lookouts and the OD, like fire-men sliding down the brass pole in a fire station.

There's no such command as "Crash dive," as the motion picture studios would have us believe. Every dive is made as quickly as possible. That's the only way to achieve speed and perfection. All you have to do is kick out the corks, let in the water, and down you go.

Technically, here's what really happens. Even before the conning tower hatch is shut, water is admitted into the main ballast tanks by opening a series of vents. Diesel engines are shut down and men in the maneuvering room cut over for propulsion to the electric motors fed by tons of huge battery cells.

Air pressure is built up within the boat to test her airtightness, and the main induction, which provides fresh air for the engines and the rest of the submarine, is shut. When the proper vents are closed, a "green board" shows up on the "Christmas Tree" panel in the control room. This consists of a series of small lights — green denoting closed and red for open — which automatically show the condition of valves, vents, and hatches. It's one of the greatest safety factors aboard.

Bow and stern planes resembling fins are always rigged for diving while the boat is underway. These regulate the depth and the angle of dive, just as the elevators of an airplane regulate its altitude and angle of climb.

When the captain decides just how deep he wants to go, the diving officer levels off by using the auxiliary tanks amidships, the regular trimming tanks, and the bow and stern tanks to adjust his trim. Our main ballast tanks are located outside the pressure hull, as are the negative and safety tanks, used to speed surfacing or diving.

Griffith waited 20 minutes then brought the sub to

periscope depth for a look-see. The coast was clear and he called out over the squawk box, "All compartments stand by to surface."

Machinist's mates stood by ready to start the Diesel engines and open the main induction valve. In the control room they checked the closed vents, while in the upper control station in the conning tower lookouts prepared to climb topside as soon as the boat broke water.

"Diving officer ready to surface," announced the OD, and the deafening Klaxon honked three times — the signal for surfacing.

Powerful pumps blew out tons of water from the main ballast and bow buoyancy tanks, and the boat shot upward and forward rapidly. I could hear the rush of water splashing down the sides of the hull as we surfaced, opened the main induction, and switched back to the Diesels. Meanwhile the plane had disappeared. Griffith presumed it was based at one of the many Jap airfields on Formosa.

Fifteen minutes after the close call, religious services were held in the crowded crew's quarters in the after battery room. Men in khakis and dungarees sat on the edge of bunks; others stood and braced themselves against the rolling of the submarine. There wasn't even room for a chair for the captain.

Yeoman 1st class, James J. Brantley, who prepared the order of service, delivered the Call to Worship, Psalm 122:1, then we sang Hymn 19 (Come Thou Almighty King) with Comdr. Griffith's clear, baritone voice standing out above all the rest.

Brantley, an ordained Mormon minister in civilian life, read the Scripture Lesson, Psalm 95, and was followed by torpedoman 2nd class, William Ireland, who read the Lord's Prayer. After the singing of the Navy Hymn, quartermaster 3rd class, Adrianus J. Schellinkhout, former president of the Youth League at his church in Midlothian, Ill., delivered the sermon, "A Light Through the Darkness." The non-sectarian service was a tremendously stimulating one, and a vivid demonstration of what American men could do thousands of miles from home without the spiritual leadership of a chaplain.

Religious services were inaugurated recently, after Comdr. Griffith had posted this notice on the bulletin board:

The following is quoted from a patrol report (they sank 35,000 tons):

"There is a definite desire from a large percentage of our submarine crews to have a weekly religious service. This has been amply proved by the several boats that have Sunday services. Knowing the help and comfort these services provide, the commanding officer of the USS............ recommends that all submarines give proper consideration to having a religious service of one form or another each Sunday."

It is proposed that this boat set aside a part of each Sunday for a short service. Since we do not have a chaplain aboard to push this work our own efforts will determine its strength.

The skipper doubled as preacher at the first service and everyone who wasn't on watch attended. He described religion, as defined by Dr. Brown of St. John's College in Annapolis, as, "A feeling of responsibility for things as they ought to be." Griffith added, "That, too, means living in accordance with your conscience; and doing and being what you know is right. If you don't, you are doomed to spiritual darkness and great unhappiness."

I have great respect for the captain; he's a real leader. He doesn't attend services as a spectator, but leads the singing and the prayers with a guiding voice. He is a credit to the service and an inspiration to his men.

Brantley, who directed today's service, carries a large religious library with him. Before joining the Bullhead, he completed four war patrols on the Tinosa. He hails from a family of 10 children. His father was one of seven, his mother one of five, and his wife, Staff Sgt. Mellanie Brantley, with the WAC in Paris, was one of seven children.

The Sunday service had scarcely ended when we were busy again. The radar operator picked up another enemy plane and we dove at once.

3

Monday, March 26 — There is nothing more monotonous and boring than idle time and unpleasant companions. Fortunately, the Bullhead's officers and enlisted men are most amiable and companionable, and everyone gets along remarkably well, despite the cramped quarters and the constant cruising day after day.

But submariners are plagued with an excess of idle time, since a war patrol is now 90 per cent boredom and patient waiting, and only 10 per cent action. That is, if you're really lucky. It's well-nigh impossible to exercise and work the kinks out of your muscles, although a Negro steward's mate, Percy Johnson, of Dayton, Ohio, finds space to shadow box after dinner. He also does deep knee bends and chins himself on the frame of a bunk in the tenebrosity of the forward torpedo room.

He boxed for the Y. M. C. A. in Dayton, and had planned to challenge the former welterweight boxing champion, Al Roth, until he learned that Roth had been wounded during the Army's campaign for the Philippines.

My only complaint is insomnia. I find it impossible to get tired enough to sleep. First, I eat a light breakfast, read for a while, nibble at lunch (like a walrus, says the skipper), work a couple of hours at my typewriter, then just lounge around and read some more until dinner. After the evening meal, more reading and then into my hard sack for a restless, seemingly perpetual night. Being more or less accustomed to a terra firma routine of considerable activity and working under pressure — not the air pressure bled into a submarine — this sudden about-face has become particularly difficult to assimilate.

In a few days I have read more books than during the past three years. Several were about those ill-fated submarines, the S-51 and the S-4, which sank off the New England coast in the twenties.

All submariners are assiduous readers. One of the most sought after books is the World Almanac, the boat's bible, used nightly in the crew's mess to settle arguments and bets concerning facts and figures. Two weeks after the 1945 edition was added to the library, the volume looked as if it had been run over by a heavy tank.

The Bullhead reached her lifeguard station off the southern tip of Formosa early this morning and submerged for five and one-half hours, until a handful of P-38's arrived from the Philippines to cover us for a while. After they left to return to their bases, we dove again and remained in hiding until sundown, when Comdr. Griffith decided to poke around Takao Harbor in search of enemy shipping.

"We'll surface now," he said, "and act as if we owned the bloody place."

During the moonlit night, we squeezed to within seven miles of the busy city of 75,000, practically daring any patrol craft to come out for a fight. But we didn't see one sign of the enemy.

The skipper is hopeful, however. He has just posted the following notice on the bulletin board:

I AM OFFERING ONE QUART (NOT A FIFTH) OF LIQUOR TO THE FIRST MAN TO SIGHT A SHIP WE SINK.

My speedy offer to stand a lookout watch, and possibly qualify for the bottle, was not accepted.

March 27 — It was about two o'clock this morning, while we were charging batteries on the surface near

Formosa, that a Jap twin engine bomber came in on us fast and low, having sighted and followed our unmistakable wake in the bright moonlight. Earl Hackman, who had the watch, described the beat of the plane's engines as advising him to, "Take her down. Take her down. Take her down."

And take her down, he did. He ordered the bridge cleared and sounded the diving alarm. The first lookout, Fred J. Jewell, of Roanoke, Va., was in such a hurry to get down that he struck his head against the steel overhang above the hatch and knocked himself out, Hackman, a balding 1943 graduate of the Naval Academy, helped him below. Two other lookouts followed, then the quartermaster and the OD, a split second before the sea lapped at the deckwork of the bridge.

It's an uncomfortable feeling to lie in your sack during a dive, especially if you sleep, as I do, with your head toward the bow. While the boat noses down rapidly, you can hear water gurgling in the flooding tanks. There's an eerie crackling and creaking throughout the boat as both the depth and pressure increase. Your head is lower than your feet, and you experience a sensation of falling.

You begin to wonder, "When the devil are they going to level off?" Also, "How many fathoms have we below us?" And, "Are there any uncharted pinnacles in this area?" Then comes the reassuring hissing of the flooding after tanks. You come out of the dive, and soon your body is level again. Everyone breathes a sigh of relief.

March 28 — Planes drove us down twice during the night. Time drags interminably for me, although we've been out only a week. But time doesn't drag for the two thirds of the crew attempting to qualify in submarines. Even after they have been graduated from Submarine School at New London, and have served aboard old O, R, and S boats, their education is only beginning when they are assigned to a fleet submarine such as the Bullhead.

Every enlisted man and officer must qualify in all departments of an underseas craft within six months, or after two war patrols, or risk transfer to a surface ship. Every man must know the others' jobs. This means a cook must be able to stand engine room and sound watches, and a yeoman must know enough to substitute for radio and torpedo room watchstanders.

First, they prepare a voluminous notebook with the answers to several hundred questions and draw a score of diagrams tracing the various pumping, electrical and fuel systems and other installations in the boat. Then a qualified officer takes the applicant on a tour of the sub, questioning him about the operation and purpose of anything and everything he may see. This trip sometimes lasts two and one-half hours or even longer and is followed by a shorter final exam given by the executive officer. Only when an applicant passes the above tests is he considered fully qualified in submarines and entitled to advance in rate.

Every man aboard, whether qualified or not, receives submarine pay — an extra 50 per cent of his normal base pay — for this dangerous duty. However, enlisted men cannot wear dolphins on the sleeves of their jumpers, and officers are not awarded their gold dolphin insignia, until they qualify.

Until about 15 years ago, the Navy paid a one dollar bonus for every dive up to a maximum of $15 a month. Before the war, extra pay for submarine personnel amounted to $25 a month to compensate for the inconveniences of crowded living and for purchasing enough extra clothing to last throughout a long patrol.

March 29 — We're still standing by on our dreary lifeguard assignment. None of the fly-fly boys has been shot down in our area, and we're happy for them.

I spent 15 minutes topside for the first time in four days.

I learned that the boat's namesake, the bullhead, is of the catfish family; it is similar to the horned pout found in New England lakes and ponds. According to those learned in piscatology, the bullhead prefers warm and weedy waters, prowls along the bottom and feeds day and night on snails, crustaceans, and bivalve mollusks.

As for this Bullhead, it, too, prefers warm water and prowls along the bottom.

4

Modern fleet submarines, with their mass of intricate pipes, valves, dials, gauges, tanks, motors, engines, and 250 locked receptacles, are the most compact and crowded pieces of fighting machinery in use. They have room for everything — except claustrophobiacs, a brig and a mistake. And they're a conglomeration only until you straighten them out in your mind.

Standard equipment on these craft are radios with speakers in all compartments, automatic record players, an electric washing machine, a sewing machine, and a pair of hair clippers usually wielded by a man very suddenly designated as "ship's barber." There are three showers (though water conservation rules limit us to a feeble sprinkling once every five or six days), a sunlamp (rarely used), a popular ice cream freezing unit, and a 16-millimeter sound motion picture projector. And let's not forget to mention the 10 torpedo tubes, a five inch deck gun and the 20- and 40-millimeter guns.

Perhaps the best feature aboard is the complete air conditioning system that maintains the inside temperature at approximately 75 degrees, although the outside water temperature usually reaches the high 80's in the Pacific. This marvelous system dries and cools the air, keeping everyone surprisingly comfortable even when we are submerged for 10 to 14 hours, and also prevents dehydration of the boat's giant batteries.

The air conditioning plant is so efficient that smoking is permitted everywhere, except in the magazines and the lower motor room. What, at first, makes you break out in a cold sweat and feel weak in the knees, is seeing a man light a cigarette and lean casually against a long torpedo complete with warhead. It's perfectly safe, however. So they tell me, anyway.

Let's take a walk through the double-hulled Bullhead to get our bearings. She is 311 feet 9 inches long, with a beam of 27 feet 2 inches, and a displacement of 1,525 tons, about one ninth of which are batteries. She can attain a speed of better than 20 knots on the surface, about 8 or 9 submerged. She cost in the neighborhood of $8,000,000 ready to go to sea.

We'll begin at the bow and stroll toward the stern. The first compartment, and a mighty important one, is the forward torpedo room where six tubes can spit out torpedoes at enemy ships. There's a small sign with red letters hanging on each tube, DANGER TOR-PEDO IN TUBE, so you know we're ready for action.

On both sides of this compartment are three-decker bunks, whose occupants snooze unconcernedly over and beside part of the reserve supply of greased 21 foot torpedoes. Clothes lockers are built in above the up-permost sacks, and snapped onto the frame of each bunk is a ditty bag containing shaving equipment and other toilet articles. Here, as in every compartment, you'll find generators and other complicated equipment plus one of our two escape hatches. Sound gear is located in the after end of the room.

There isn't much clearance, so duck your head when you step through the watertight door to the forward battery room. Below deck is a series of 126 huge battery cells, each weighing 1,630 pounds, the largest in daily use. At the right is the wardroom galley, a minute cubicle with deck area measuring two by five feet, serving 10 of us.

Next comes the wardroom, identified by a wooden sign: THE ELITE DINETTE. It is here that the only semblance of formality can be found aboard a submarine, the wearing of shirts — sometimes not tucked in — by officers at chow. Ordinarily they run around clad only in tropical shorts.

I can't pass up describing the wardroom in detail. The deck space measures only six by eight feet. It's the captain's office, the navigator's office; in fact, everybody's office. Even I horn in occasionally to use my portable. This is where the officers gormandize, where they engage in acey ducey and cribbage tournaments, where they listen to a squealing radio, and settle the great economic problems of the day. The two leather chairs and the transoms never get a chance to cool off.

Two of us sleep in here. On the long sides are green leather transoms, each seating three men. The back of one is converted after dinner into an upper berth; the seat serving as a lower. The upper one is fairly comfortable, but the lower (mine) has no spring and is as uninviting and incommodious as a country outhouse during a 20 below zero blizzard.

I need a shoehorn to squeeze between the table top and the upper bunk into my sack, and once I have completed these contortions and am safely ensconced, I intermittently scrape my elbows and lacerate my knees each time I turn from side to side. Built into the bulkhead at my feet is an automatic record changer, while towels, sheets, and spreads, part of the boat's library, and games are stuffed into lockers behind my head. Three chronometers are stored in the wardroom, along with enough navigator's charts to fill eight drawers.

On the passageway bulkhead are magazine racks, a clock, and a small photograph of a burning Japanese vessel with an American submarine's deck gun in the foreground. Below are printed these succinct words by Admiral Lockwood:

> Commanding officers must go after every ship sighted. With targets as scarce as they are, submarines must take what comes, rather than wait for something better, and must relentlessly pursue all contacts.

A large chart of the Western Pacific has been framed and hung on the outboard bulkhead, while on the ceiling are mounted two fans, two fluorescent light fixtures, a large red lamp used after sundown, and three loud speakers for the boat's communication system, record player and radio. Then there's another set of eight drawers for glasses, cups and saucers, silverware, and some of our personal gear. If the room seems a bit crowded, well, that's the impression I am trying to convey.

Directly across the passageway from the galley is a tiny officers' shower. Next to it is a four man stateroom with folding Pullman washstand; then the captain's cabin with room for only one chair. At the foot of his narrow bunk is a depth gauge and compass repeater, while on the bulkhead hangs a direct telephone to the bridge. The entire cabin is the size of a small closet.

Now comes a three bunk officers' cabin and the chiefs' room with bunks for five; across from it, the yeoman's microscopic office where I do most of my writing. Everything does double duty in this pigeonhole. The stool serves as a wastebasket and is, furthermore, the hanging place for two wooden clip boards. It's incredible how many things have been crammed into so little space. As one wag put it, "A submarine is so crowded we have to use condensed milk in the galley."

Through another watertight door we enter the nerve center of the Bullhead, the main control room, where all the diving controls are situated. Directly below is the pump room; directly above is the conning tower with an upper control room for operating under water, twin periscopes, steering gear, and radionic equipment. At the after end of the compartment is the crowded radio "shack."

The after battery room houses another 126 batteries below deck, also the refrigerators for meat and other perishable food. In the crew's galley, much smaller than most apartment kitchenettes, three men prepare the chow for the boat's present complement of 84 men. Sometimes the cooks perform culinary miracles here; then again they occasionally murder meals in a most brutal manner.

Next comes the forward engine room with two main Diesel engines, the submersible's main lighting and ventilating systems, and twin evaporators capable of producing 1,500 gallons of fresh water daily. Two other main engines and an auxiliary are located in the after engine room, along with the fuel system and the air conditioning unit. While on surface, the Diesels are also used to charge batteries.

Another important compartment is the maneuvering room where you'll find the main power controls. Electrician's mates on watch here switch from Diesels to electric motors and reduction gears with long levers whenever the boat is submerged. Below deck stand the four main motors and reduction gears, operating the shafts to the two propellers.

Eighth and last is the after torpedo room with four stern tubes and crew's quarters. All sections contain a supply of oxygen masks and carbon dioxide absorbent, while each torpedo room is stocked with enough Momsen breathing lungs for the entire crew, in case the boat should become disabled while submerged and the men are in a position to use the escape hatches.

March 30 — We are back off Formosa where things are so quiet that the old man authorized movies for the first time. Later, we received orders to depart for a new station off Hong Kong.

5

Saturday, March 31 — While en route to the China Coast, the skipper requested permission from ComSub-Pac to hold gun firing practice with a small Chinese island, now occupied by the Japs, as the target.

"Permission granted," came the word from head-quarters and there was feverish activity by the gunnery crew.

Now it is 3:30 a.m., and we are laying 900 yards off Pratas Reef, a circular coral reef enclosing a possible junk anchorage, about midway between Formosa and Hong Kong. According to the old chart we have, it's a tiny claw-shaped isle with radio and weather stations, and a few small buildings at one end.

Someone jokingly attempts to persuade Comdr. Griffith to send a landing party* ashore, but he shakes his head. It's inadvisable, he says, because we don't have anything except a rubber boat. And the wide fringing reef surrounding Pratas would quickly rip that to shreds, if we tried to use it as a landing craft.

Over the squawk box echoes, "Battle stations — gun action!" There's a scuffling of sandaled feet through-out the boat. This is the Bullhead's first shore shelling assignment and the gun crews are determined to make it successful. They quickly man the 20- and 40-milli-meters, and the big five incher.

Earl Hackman, the torpedo and gunnery officer, yells

*About June 1, 1945, following Griffith's report of few signs of life on Pratas, the submarine Bluegill, commanded by Comdr. Eric L. Barr, Jr., sent a landing party ashore in a special boat. They didn't find any Japs but there was evidence that they had cleared out only a short while before. The Bluegill force destroyed the radio and weather station equipment and blew up an oil dump.

out, "Range, nine hundred yards. Scale, five zero two. Bearing, zero nine zero relative."

The sea is calm and a setting moon illuminates the scene, though not too brilliantly. The command is given and the first couple of rounds land to the left of the target.

"Bearing, zero nine two," corrects Hackman. Then a curt, "Fire!"

This time we are on target. For six minutes we hurl round after round at those Japanese installations ashore. Most of the shells land within the target area; one scores a direct hit on a building. The Japs don't return our fire and we cannot see any lights among the shacks. As soon as the last shell hits the ground and splashes coral dust, we are high-tailing it for the open sea.

"I didn't realize our five inchers would illuminate the place so brightly," Griffith admits later. "That was the first time I had ever shelled a beach. I figured that six minutes' shelling would be just about enough. It would take the Japs at least that long to wake up and man their guns, if any, and by the time the last shell hit the shore we could be on our merry way. Knock on wood, it worked out that way."

In a few hours, at breakfast, everyone was in for another experience. One I'm sure I'll never forget. As usual, I was the first man at the wardroom table. Not because I was a chow hound, but because I slept there. Tex Simms always snoozed in his sack until nine so we kept the red lights on until that time.

One of the stewards brought in a dark concoction which I probed without success. Finally, with the utmost bravery, I tasted it, swallowed a mouthful with difficulty, and turned a revealing flashlight on the plate. The menu specified "minced meat on toast." But our new cook had heated up mincemeat — the kind that goes into pies — and poured it over slices of bread. I couldn't leave the wardroom. Instead, I waited until all the officers came in for breakfast, and gleefully watched for the expressions of surprise and nausea that swept their faces after they tasted the strange combination.

The captain screamed for the steward's mate when he tasted the mess.

"Goddammit," he yelled. "I don't know what this awful mixture is, but don't ever serve it again!!"

The shelling was still the number one topic of conversation when, midway through jello this evening, a messenger rapped on the wardroom bulkhead to inform the captain that our lookouts had sighted an unidentifiable object on the horizon. He leaped from his chair, as if awakened with a hotfoot, sped to the bridge, and returned a few moments later with field glasses hanging from his neck.

"Looks like a two masted schooner," he announced, reaching for a cigarette. "I've rung up full speed and we're closing to investigate."

I went topside, but as soon as I stepped foot in the open a lookout cried, "Plane on the port quarter, sir."

An officer and I tumbled down the ladder to thin out an already crowded bridge in case we had to dive. "Only a bird," someone sang out a moment later, so back we went.

By this time we could make out a high sterned, dingy sailed Chinese junk; a half mile closer to us were four small black dories bobbing in the water. We raised our colors and steered a course taking us within 50 yards of one of the small boats. Its three skinny occupants wore straw coolie hats and were pulling up fishing nets, apparently utterly indifferent to our presence.

.The bottom of their boat was ankle deep with white fish. The men continued to putter with their lines and hooks. One might have thought a snooping submarine was an everyday occurrence.

Convinced that they were harmless Chinese fishermen, we moved on to the next dory. The skipper waved a greeting to the haggard looking men in it; they removed their hats in the same friendly manner that Filipinos did, and waved back at us.

The dazzling sun, a great reddish ball of fire, disappeared below the twilight haze as we caught up with the remaining boats whose occupants were now paddling furiously toward their odd looking mother craft. Maybe they had heard the call to chow.

The picturesque junk, in silhouette, reminded me of an artist's conception of Columbus' "Santa Maria." She didn't carry any colors but seemed to be innocent enough. Her fore and mainmasts carried reinforced, homemade fiber sails, practically a certain indication that she was Chinese. The Japs usually operated with new cloth sails and an auxiliary engine.

Fish were drying on the raised poop deck. The women and children aboard showed no signs of fear or concern and, apparently, were just a few of the thousands, perhaps millions. of Chinese who live on crowded boats at sea, or on the great rivers, and eke out a bare subsistence fishing and trading their dried fish for rice.

We waved again to the junk's passengers and returned to our former course. An hour later four lights were reported on the horizon. These, too, belonged to junks; in all probability to junks that had sailed from Canton and Hong Kong. Soon we were practically surrounded by them and, at nine p.m., our position was only 12 miles from Hong Kong.

During the night we received a dispatch from the Blackfish advising us that she was submerging to attack. An hour later she identified her target as a Japanese hospital ship and went on her way without molesting the mercy vessel.

The Japs are believed to be using as many as 25 "hospital" ships, certainly a suspiciously large number since they haven't had many wounded men to evacuate. We all know most of their fanatical troops always fight to their death.

While it is quite possible the Japs may be transporting troops and supplies in the purported hospital ships, according to international law there isn't a thing we can do about it so long as they identify themselves properly with a large Red Cross, steam fully lighted on a straight course at night, and do not mount guns. Our submarines have specific orders NOT to attack hospital ships.

We had a treat the other afternoon in the flickering of a five year old Kay Kyser feature, "You'll Find Out," as projected on a swinging sheet in the forward torpedo room. We sat on the edge of bunks and used torpedoes for back rests. The skipper alone was honored with a chair.

Enlisted men see movies about three afternoons a week, the hours being changed to give different watch-standers an opportunity to attend the cinema. It's their only relaxation on patrol, except for sack drill. We have two dozen 16-millimeter features aboard, from one to five years old; but any movie is better than none, especially if a man hasn't seen it before.

* * * * *

Comdr. Griffith passed along this story told to him by another submarine commander who swore it was absolutely true. While evacuating an American mother and her small Filipino-American son from the Philippines, the sub skipper related seeing the youngster alternately feed at his mother's breast and puff at a long black cigar. Despite the inconceivability of the incident, Griffith vouched for the veracity of his colleague.

6

Easter Sunday, April 1 — The Pacific Thought and Cultural Society met at 8:30 this morning around the breakfast table, under the dim red glow of wardroom lights, only an hour from the coast of China. In attendance were the charter members: the skipper, his executive officer and navigator, 26 year old Lieut. Keith R. Phillips of Los Angeles, the first lieutenant, Lieut. (jg) Paul A. Gossett, of Waynesville, N. C., and I.

"I never could understand why they ever serve flapjacks," grumbled Comdr. Griffith, jabbing viciously at his plate with a fork. "Hell, I can hardly spear these fugitives from a rubber factory. They're practically raw."

Then aside to the pantry he called, "Bring me my coffee."

"I like bran pancakes, golden brown, and well cooked," I chimed in.

"Wheatcakes with bran really have body to them," added Phillips, better known by the crew as "Field Day" Phillips for his many work orders. "My mother sometimes adds a little corn meal to the batter. She mentioned something about better flavor, I think."

Gossett, a short affable Southerner, complained about his inability to buy maple syrup at home because, as the storekeeper explained it, "Most of the supply is going to the armed forces."

"I've never seen any aboard ship," said Gossett. "All we ever got was watery cane syrup, just like lubricating oil but with far less flavor."

The next topic to be bandied about was men's neckties, which we unanimously agreed was an undeserved major curse on mankind. Gossett told of the first time he forced his younger brother to submit to wearing a noose around his neck.

"I practically had to lasso the poor kid," he chuckled. "After tying the knot and pushing it up to his collar, he was unable to move for four hours. Most amazing sight we ever did see. He thought he was tied to a tree."

The captain discussed the discomforts of wearing ties back at Pearl Harbor and in the States, after going without them for so many months in forward areas.

"I'd like to tighten a noose around the neck of the guy who originated the abominable style," he added bitterly.

I described my violent dislike of heavy overcoats. Comments by the others proved we were in accord.

"I'll never forget the heavy dress coats we wore at the Academy," recalled the captain. "Particularly when we had to march a few miles through Baltimore, Boston, and other cities to football games. Those things must have weighed nearly 20 pounds. Man, we were really exhausted and round shouldered at the end of the day, especially if we carried a bottle in our pockets.

"I can't stand vests, either," he added, "but I haven't had any occasion to wear civilian clothes since the war began. In pre-war days, we wore uniforms only aboard ship and switched to civvies whenever going ashore. It was a most satisfactory arrangement. Before Pearl Harbor, civilians would gaze at a man in uniform as if he were a freak from a side show."

Although I dislike vests, I was forced to admit I had worn one intermittently during the past two years when in the office, merely to have a place to store my pencils and pen.

The sociological discussion moved on inexorably to women. Gossett informed us with a drawl of his marriage last August. The skipper is a veteran at the game, having been married nine years. He boasted that he could cook better than his wife, and added with a laugh, "She won't admit it and that's what keeps her on her toes."

"I haven't been home long enough to find out whether Peggy can cook," I said. "I left for the Pacific after being married only 16 days. There are a few dishes I like to prepare myself, though. Chile con carne, spaghetti and meat sauce, and super salads."

The captain didn't think it was wise to let some wives discover you could cook. "Might tend to encourage them to depend on your help," he said. "Of course, if your wife can't cook, you've got to be able to prepare something or starve."

Phillips, still a bachelor, could not add a word on the subject.

All of us agreed vociferously that women's long, red fingernails are particular offensive to men. The mere sight of them moves some males to violence and induces others to shut up like a clam.

"I'm convinced after all these years (he's only 33) that women dress only to impress other women and to outdo one another, not to please their husbands," declared Comdr. Griffith. "Hell, I've yelled myself blue in the face entreating Nell to discard bright, clawlike fingernails, but she persists in wearing them."

"Mine quit painting her nails when I complained," I said meekly.

"You haven't been married long enough to understand those things," advised "Mr. Anthony" Gossett. "A woman might discontinue using bright polish for a few days, but she'll return to it again."

"Yes," agreed Phillips. "Why at this very moment your wife is probably dabbing on the brightest red polish available."

"I don't think Peggy would do that," I retorted.

The others laughed heartily. "Dreamer!" they scoffed. And the meeting adjourned.

* * * * *

It's a beautiful, warm Easter Sunday and we're cruising peacefully off Hong Kong in smooth water. (American forces landed on Okinawa this morning.) Simple divine services were held at two o'clock in the forward torpedo room with 24 men present. Missing were beautiful flowers and smartly attired women.

The crew's Easter raiment consisted of the usual duds, khakis, greens and dungarees; except for the skipper, who replaced his tropical shorts with long trousers, and divested his faded sport shirt in favor of a long sleeved khaki shirt complete with a commander's silver insignia and dolphins. The only women present were the shapely pinups who looked on silently from the bulkheads and lockers.

7

On no other type of ship can one find the close liaison between officers and enlisted men, and the staunch camaraderie found on a submarine. Life here is easygoing and unrestrained.

This sub's spirit of comradeship dates back several months to the gala ship's party given in New London and attended by the officers and the crew, their wives and sweethearts, and is still going strong. The program continued all the way out here with baseball games, swimming and beer parties at the several ports of call.

There also exists a closer bond between a submarine's captain and his officers than can be found on larger ships. Of necessity, the skipper sits in the wardroom at chow with the other stripers.

On practically every ship larger than a PC, the captain estranges himself in conformity with the old Navy custom of eating and living alone, and divides his time between the bridge and his tiny sea cabin when underway. On battleships and aircraft carriers, only a few of the enlisted men know the captain by sight.

A submarine is similar to the great melting pot of New York City, where a hundred different races intermingle amid the hustle and bustle of a great metropolis. Aboard this craft, the officers, chiefs and other enlisted men rub elbows with one another, with no gulf and little differentiation between them. If anything, I believe the enlisted personnel sometimes enjoy an advantage where food is concerned.

The skipper is king, none the less, but a sort of democratic king. He knows every man's name and some of his background. Every man knows the captain and respects him.

FIRST WAR PATROL

Only one regular inspection has been held aboard the Bullhead since her commissioning, although other warships usually hold a captain's inspection every Saturday morning. A sub is too small a place in which to hide dirt in a corner; besides, the men take personal pride in keeping all compartments shining and spotless on their own initiative.

At the end of each war patrol, a sub returns for an overhaul to a tender at either Subic Bay, Guam, Saipan, Midway, Pearl Harbor, or Fremantle, with the Australian base rating an unanimous first in desirability. The entire crew leaves the boat in a body and moves to a submarine rest camp for two weeks' recuperation. (In Australia and Hawaii, they live in hotels.) Fresh food for all camps, as well as for hospitals, is acquired with top priority. During this refit period a relief crew moves aboard the sub to paint, make repairs and get her in tip-top condition for another rigorous patrol.

Who are the men of this crew? They're just ordinary lads who might live down your street. For example, let's consider torpedoman 2nd class, Stanley J. Chalecki, a tall, raw-boned youngster from Worcester, Mass., who went directly into the Navy from the High School of Commerce and has served four years. At 20, he is a veteran of five war patrols on an old S-boat.

Those nearly obsolete craft had neither air conditioning nor adequate heating facilities in the early days. They were uncomfortably cold in the Aleutians, unbearably hot in the South Pacific.

"We were lucky because our boat was the first of her class to be equipped with air conditioning," Chalecki explained, stroking a two inch beard. "On our first two patrols to Cape St. George and Tulagi, the skipper destroyed two merchantmen, but we really hit the jackpot during the third run.

"It was about 7:30 in the morning off Rabaul. A few of us were shooting the breeze in the control room.

We were discussing what we'd do if we ever encountered the Japanese Fleet. I told the boys I'd fire fish in all directions.

" 'Well, here's your big chance, you armchair admirals,' interrupted the officer of the deck, who was peering through the periscope. 'Tell the captain I've sighted two Jap cruisers!'

"We laughed," Chalecki went on, "thinking it was a gag since the OD had overhead our conversation. But we jumped when he cried out, 'Jee-sus Christ!! Tell the old man we've got four Jap cruisers now. They're heading south in a column, bearing, one six five, range, ten thousand five hundred yards!'

"Those S-boats had only four torpedo tubes so we had to make every shot count. The skipper closed the warships, then waited for the last one to come along. He gave her four fish. Every one hit the Nip. We felt several explosions, and watched great clouds of smoke and steam fill the sky as the stern of the ship started down. It was all over in seven minutes."

Joseph W. Jones, 24, electrician's mate 1st class, is a fugitive from a cattle ranch in Rule, Texas. This red bearded submariner has completed nine war patrols, any one of them hot enough to make a man wish he had never thought of leaving the range and going to sea.

Jones was in Manila on December 8, 1941. He saw the terrible destruction inflicted on our naval base and ships at Cavite. But his most thrilling experience occurred on the 42nd day of a war patrol on the USS Seal near the Palau Islands. The sub had picked up a convoy of eight small freighters about 10 a.m., and submerged to periscope depth to make her attack.

Two merchantmen went down for the ten-count from torpedoes. Somehow, just then, the submarine broached for a couple of minutes amid a noisy froth of bubbles. The Japs couldn't help but see the underwater raider and sent one ship over to ram her. But the sub was brought under control again and they began to dive the boat; a few seconds too late, however. The Jap ship struck.

"There was a frightening clatter of scraping and ripping metal," said Jones. "It sounded as if our boat were being torn to pieces. The skipper couldn't see light through the periscopes, so he knew they had been flattened or sheared off. Then water started to pour into the after battery room.

"To top it all, the Japs dropped from 30 to 40 ashcans all around us and really rattled our teeth. We stayed below all day and didn't surface until dark. Evidently the Jap freighter had also suffered damage, because, later, we found several 100 pound sacks of rice jammed into our wrecked superstructure."

Radioman Kenneth R. Cook, of Old Greenwich, Conn., had the unnerving experience of being on deck when his submarine began to submerge. He was aboard the ill-fated Wahoo in the Yellow Sea at the time, busily greasing some gear near the bow. The sub picked up a radar contact, later found to be false, and began to dive. Cook hadn't heard the OD shout, "Clear the bridge!" and did not realize what was happening until the bow dipped under the water and his feet got wet.

"I could only think, 'I can't speak Japanese,'" Cook said. "Believe me, I was scared stiff until I heard the sub blow ballast and saw the conning tower hatch open for me."

Cook told me of another man who lived through a similar experience on the Sturgeon; a seaman 2nd class, named Peak, who was striking for a deck rate. He was standing lookout watch at the time. The skipper yelled, "Clear the bridge!" but Peak didn't hear it. Everyone else scrambled below; the quartermaster tried to dog the hatch when the boat was starting down, only to feel the handle being twisted in the opposite direction.

Finally, he realized that someone was trapped topside and notified the captain. When the boat blew back to surface, the conning tower gang found a terrified and wet Peak clinging to a periscope. He immediately requested his rate be changed to fireman and never went topside again during that patrol.

Cook was associated with a New York advertising agency before joining the Navy. He served on the aircraft carrier Lexington at Pearl Harbor, then volunteered for submarines so he might spend his liberty from Submarine School in New London at his home. During his first patrol on the Wahoo, she destroyed a large Jap troopship carrying an estimated 6,000 men and was awarded a Presidential Unit Citation.

One of our cooks, Robert J. Wiemann, of Arlington, Minn., was a junior at Gustavus Adolphus College when he decided to see the world. He had never boiled water before volunteering for underwater prowling. Now, with the help of three mess cooks chosen from the crew each month to clean the galley, set up tables and wash dishes, Wiemann cooks for 85 men in a small galley with a tiled deck area of 2½ by 7 feet. Within his reach are a deep fat fryer, two electric ranges, an electric mixer, a two gallon coffee urn, and a modicum of storage space.

Carl W. Piatt, our capable baker from Chicago, sweat in a midwestern steel mill until he signed up for submarines to tangle with dough and batter and the Japs. He bakes 24 loaves of bread daily, plus 16 to 20 pies whenever they are on the menu. Four huge tins of frosted cake disappear for dessert four times a week, and once a week we can be certain of excellent cinnamon buns, coffee cake, or corn bread.

Piatt says he enjoys his work, but the resulting compliments please him more than anything else. Occasionally he provides ambrosia in the shape of delectable chocolate cream puffs or luscious pineapple upside-down cake. He achieves marvelous results, despite the rolling of the boat that sometimes splashes batter out of the baking pan. But whenever the guns are fired, his cakes and muffins suffer accordingly by resembling pancakes.

A good baker and a good cook are two important requisites toward achieving a happy submarine crew. Next to resting in the sack, eating is the greatest pastime on these crowded craft. Maybe eating is the more important. Anyway, filling a man's stomach to the contentment level with palatable food will go a long way toward keeping morale at a high level, just as the sages declare the way to a man's heart is through his stomach.

One of our men, machinist's mate 3rd class, Paul L. Rogers, 21, of Carterville, Ill., is married to an Australian girl whom he met at an Australian high school graduation dance. They were finally married in June, 1944, over the objections of the Australian government and several relatives.

The man with the greatest number of patrols to his credit is husky William E. Short, 23, torpedoman 1st class, of Jackson Heights, N. Y., who has been on 12 submarine war patrols, including an abnormally long 76 day run on the USS Swordfish. This is his fifth year in the Navy.

Short was aboard the Swordfish in the Philippines when war broke out. On December 8, 1941, he said, the sub left Corregidor with a list of distinguished passengers that included the late President of the Philippines, Manuel Quezon, his wife and three children, Vice President Osmeno, a Philippine and an American general, and a Philippine Army chaplain.

"We sailed at six," Short related. "About five hours later we got a contact that turned out to be a Japanese seaplane tender. Everyone was excited because of the urgency of our mission and wondered what the captain would do. He fooled them and took time out to fire two torpedoes that hit the tender."

The Swordfish continued on to Panay where she sent her passengers ashore in rubber boats. She sped back to Corregidor to pick up the American High Commissioner, his family, and staff.

"Unfortunately we were then under strict orders not to fire at anything," Short continued. "While ferrying the officials to Australia, we had a chance to knock off a Jap carrier and the temptation was terrific. Down under, we took aboard flour, beans, salt, and other supplies for the trapped American and Filipino force resisting the Japs on tiny Corregidor. A couple of days out, we heard of their fall, so the skipper returned to Australia and unloaded the chow. We took on more torpedoes and left for a war patrol off Siam and Hainan."

Fred J. Jewell, quartermaster 2nd class, made two patrols on the Peto, one of which was a thrilling reconnaissance trip to Guadalcanal in the early days of the war. At midnight, four bushy haired natives of the island, two Australian soldiers, and 14 U. S. Marines went ashore from the sub in rubber boats. They returned the next day, bearing souvenirs and telling of killing several Japs during their raid; the natives even managed to sneak in a visit to their families.

"The Solomon Islanders became terribly embarrassed and blushed when they saw our snappy pin up girls," Jewell related. "And they wouldn't believe our boat traveled beneath the water. So, while returning to our base, we permitted one of them to watch a dive through the periscope. When the water splashed against the glass he screamed in terror."

Aboard for temporary duty is Stephen F. Birch, photographer's mate 1st class, of Altadena, Calif. He is equipped with a 16-millimeter motion picture camera, a 4x5 Speed Graphic, a Medalist, and an assortment of lenses. The Navy hopes to produce a film* about the Submarine Service in the same vein as "Fighting Lady."

This is the first war patrol for 19 year old John E. Coyle, of Hope, R. I., the youngest member of the crew. He's an oiler in the forward engine room. Coyle enlisted in the Navy from his third year at West Warwick Junior High.

Coyle and Rogers and Jones, and the others who comprise the crew of the Bullhead, are the same youngsters you've been accustomed to seeing behind the wheels of those crazy jalopies, swigging chocolate sodas and jitterbugging at dances like cockroaches. Out here they carry a heap of responsibility on their young shoulders.

They are engaged in a man's war; they are partners in a serious business, that of operating a submarine. They know their own job and the next man's. They're the men who are fighting and winning this war, even though some aren't old enough to vote and others cannot grow a visible beard in a month.

---

*The picture has been completed. It is titled "Silent Service" and prints may be borrowed through the Office of Public Information, Navy Department, Washington, D. C.

8

Monday, April 2 — We are only 12 miles from the South China Coast and the temptation to go ashore for a sightseeing trip is almost overwhelming. Through the early morning haze I can see Hong Kong Island, on which is located part of the Jap occupied British crown colony. The weather is clear and warm again; the sea is smooth and the sunshine makes one squint after having remained below deck so long under artificial light.

We were chatting in the wardroom after lunch when a starboard lookout reported a floating mine only a mile or so away. Comdr. Griffith rushed topside for a look, then ordered the 40-millimeter gun crew to man their weapon. I requested permission to go on the bridge and climbed up the ladder to see what went on. We were rapidly closing in on the mine. It wasn't a case of mistaken identity; even my nearsighted eyes could see the ugly detonation horns through a pair of binoculars.

"Ahead two thirds, left full rudder," ordered the skipper in a loud, clear voice. He's a stickler for men shouting their observations and commands intelligibly. A few seconds wasted in asking a repeat on a lookout's statement might mean the difference between escaping from an enemy plane's bomb and getting hit.

Soon we were only 400 yards from the bobbing yellow ball of destruction, and all engines were stopped. From the rusty appearance of the mine, we decided it had been floating in the South China Sea for many a moon. The skipper thought it had broken loose and strayed from its field during a storm. The Japs should be more damned careful with those explosive things.

Just suppose we had run into the mine at night. Someone could have been hurt.

The first shot fired was too long by 10 yards; the second too short by five. Two rounds landed only inches away from the tricky target and it ducked below the surface for a moment, then reappeared with a splash. Round number 10 struck the mine, detonating it with a mighty concussion and heaving skyward a 200 foot column of water.

Shrapnel and droplets showered all around us, disturbing the calm of the water with hundreds of tiny splashes, and bouncing a few pieces of twisted metal on our deck. Griffith confided later that he would have kept the Bullhead a bit farther away from the mine, had he realized there would be such a powerful explosion.

It's reassuring to know that we have an experienced and successful submarine commander holding the reins. I am impressed with the fact that Griff always knows what to do. There's never any hesitation or doubt in his manner; he evaluates situations rapidly, issues crisp orders with complete confidence. There is never any need for conferences concerning future courses of action.

A member of the Naval Academy's class of 1934, Griffith is a thin, auburn haired man of 145 pounds. At Annapolis, he says, his classmates called him "Red," but his hair has faded a bit since then. He's only 33 but he has lived a thousand years. His face is ruddy, thin; his nose long and his eyes pale. His appetite, I've noted, varies. Most of the time he picks at his food and eats sparingly, then sometimes he surprises us by appearing at the table with a voracious appetite and devouring a huge meal.

He gets very little extended, uninterrupted sleep such as we know it. Occasionally, between long periods of reading, he catnaps. But he is on call 24 hours a day, seven days a week. His employer, Uncle Sam, is generous but he doesn't pay overtime. Day and night, someone is always breaking in on the skipper to tell him of the sighting of vessels, lights, land, and all floating objects. Marked changes in the weather, barometer, and sea conditions are also reported to him.

A submarine's record is only as outstanding as her commander is resourceful, daring, and aggressive. At least that was true in 1942, 1943 and 1944, before Japanese merchantmen virtually disappeared from the Pacific. Comdr. Griffith's record proves that he doesn't sit around idly twiddling his thumbs. On his first war patrol as a submarine skipper aboard the USS Bowfin, he and his men sunk over 70,000 tons of enemy shipping, a record that remained in the books for two years until it was broken by Dick O'Kane with over 100,000 tons destroyed on the Tang's* final patrol off Formosa.

Griffith then sunk 21,000 tons and damaged 12,000 on his second patrol, and followed with 12,000 tons wiped out and 18,000 damaged on his third run. The Bowfin was awarded a Presidential Unit Citation for her record run; her skipper was decorated with a Navy Cross, a Silver Star, and a Gold Star (in lieu of a second Navy Cross) for that and subsequent patrols.

"Back in 1938," he recalled, "I won an expert rifleman's medal and considered myself damned lucky. Any kind of medal was difficult to get in pre-war days."

Griffith was born in Mansfield, La., where he attended public school until the 10th grade, then enlisted in the Navy on his 17th birthday. Two years later he won an appointment from the ranks to the Naval Academy. The youngster studied long hours to make up for his schooling deficiency, but he managed to find enough spare time to win letters in track and cross country,

*On the Tang's fifth and last patrol in October 1944, she sunk 13 large Japanese ships totalling approximately 107,000 tons. Comdr. O'Kane fired 24 torpedoes, 23 of which were hits, including the last defective fish which circled crazily and sunk his own craft. Nine men survived the sinking and subsequent 10 months in Jap prison camps.

turning in a fairly good two mile run in 9 min. 50 seconds.

The Louisianian was commissioned an ensign in 1934 and immediately went to sea to put in the required two years' duty with the fleet. He then signed up for Submarine School and marriage in the same week; both events having been postponed by the two year service regulation.

He completed the six month course on December 11, 1936, the same day King Edward VIII abdicated his English crown for Wally Simpson, and was assigned to the Porpoise, the first of the present fleet type submarines to be commissioned.

"We spent the next two years on the West Coast," the skipper said. "I'll never forget the day we made a dive near Monterey and the diving officer lost control of the boat through some mechanical failure. I thought we would never stop sinking. After dropping 247 feet we hit the bottom of Monterey Bay. As you can see, we finally managed to surface, but we were a bit shaky for a long while after."

Back in those days, three star Admiral Charles A. Lockwood, Jr., was a three striper and a submarine division commander. He chose the Porpoise for his flagship and Griffith first met his present superior officer at that time.

The carrot topped submariner shoved off in the Porpoise for the Pacific and served nine months at Pearl Harbor before sailing for the Philippines. As part of the Asiatic Fleet, the big sub visited Hong Kong, Shanghai, and Tsingtao, the latter port already in Japanese hands when she paid her last visit in 1940.

"There was so much friction between our boys and the Nips — scraps on the beach — that all shore liberties were cancelled for a week," Griffith said. "Everyone felt that trouble was brewing.

"In Shanghai, I was there in '40 and '41, the fashionable clubs were becoming shabby and rundown, and were about ready to fold up," the skipper went on. Then he picked up a Dunhill pipe from his tiny desk and handed it to me for examination.

"I paid five dollars for this in 1941 in Hong Kong. It was still a lively place in those days, with excellent hotels and well stocked shops. But many of the merchants were Japs; they had begun to close their businesses and return to Japan after local residents had inaugurated a personal blockade and refused to trade with them."

Mrs. Griffith was evacuated from Manila with other Navy wives in 1940, when the clouds of war began to thicken in the Far East. Asiatic Fleet submarines were kept on six hour readiness notice through 1940 and 1941, and definite tension was noted on their last runs to the China Coast.

"I left the Porpoise after 4 years 9 months service," said Griffith, "and sailed for the United States in October 1941, aboard the SS President Cleveland, along with 200 American missionaries evacuated from Japan. The Cleveland was sunk later during the North African invasion."

Back in New London, he was promoted to lieutenant and served aboard the O-2, a training sub, until January 1943, when he was sent to the Prospective Commanding Officers' School. After completing this advanced training, Griffith was ordered to Australia and assigned to the Gar for a training patrol as executive officer and navigator. This turned out to be a memorable 38 day cruise, during which the Gar more than doubled the total tonnage sunk in her previous six patrols.

Griffith was promoted to lieutenant commander and given a desk job in the submarine operations office at Perth, pending the return of a new submarine, the

Bowfin (SS-236), from her maiden patrol. He assumed command in November 1943, six days before taking her out on her second run.

The new skipper was on his way to the China Coast when he trapped four schooners in Makassar Strait (between Borneo and Celebes), and made mincemeat of them with gunfire. On Armistice Day night, he picked up two small coastal freighters laden with drums of oil, set them afire with five inch shells, and watched them hiss to their doom in a mammoth holiday celebration.

"God, but they burned beautifully," was the way he described the conflagration.

There's no end to the informality aboard a submarine, but nobody is supposed to take liberties with the captain. All other officers address each other by their first names. A new ensign, who joined the Bowfin just before she sailed, was supposedly so instructed. A few days later, he upset the boat like a nearby depth charge explosion when he met the skipper in the wardroom, slapped him on the shoulder, and greeted him with, "Hi, Walt! What's cooking?"

I've heard that Griff's unutterable surprise was followed by a burning stare rivaling an acetylene torch. The other officers had neglected to advise Junior that the first-name rule applied to everyone EXCEPT the captain.

The Bowfin arrived off Indo China in the midst of a storm that persisted for nine days and nights, and nearly forced the sub aground. For a week, the navigator had been unable to take a fix through the heavy rain and soupy low overcast. To all intents and purposes the Bowfin was lost. Then, one night, the officer of the deck reported land dead ahead. Griffith ordered a sounding taken and found but seven fathoms of water. A moment later there were only four fathoms.

"That was no fit place for us," Griffith shuddered. "I could see white water breaking 1,000 yards ahead.

Rest assured that I didn't hesitate a second. We reversed course and beat it back to the open sea in one big hurry.

"A couple of nights later, still blanketed in low, heavy overcast and pelted with buckets of rain, we were nearly run down at three a.m., by a Jap convoy of five ships escorted by two gunboats. After recovering from my surprise, I fired three fish at a large oil tanker 1,500 yards away and scored two hits. We could hear the solid thuds of our torpedoes ripping into her hull. Then there were two bluish explosions, one after the other."

The attack had disorganized the convoy, and the Bowfin moved in among the ships to knock off a transport and a freighter, in addition to the tanker. During seven hours of action Griffith scored nine bullseyes out of 11 shots, better than fair-to-middling shooting in anyone's league.

Remember, this was his first patrol as a captain; he was still supposed to be green. But two nights later, at the same position, Griffith tangled with another convoy of five ships loaded with loot from the East Indies. He fired four fish that sent a freighter to her destruction within five minutes.

Next, Griff let go with two fish toward another merchantman and scored clean hits. The Jap ship was mortally wounded but was settling too slowly to please the old man. He was swinging around to let her have two more torpedoes when the third vessel, a very large freighter, fired at the Bowfin with her deck guns. The first round screamed harmlessly overhead, but the second five inch shell landed near the after battery hatch, exploding against the superstructure.

"Just as we were hit I let the Jap freighter have our last two fish and watched her explode with a blinding burst," Griffith said. "She broke in two and I had the satisfaction of seeing the bastard go down.

"At first we weren't certain how much damage they had done to us with their gun. This is it, I thought, and I got mad as hell. The boys on the bridge said I shook my fist at the Japs but I don't remember. Just then my exec yelled up, 'Want to secure the stern tubes?' Hell, no, I told him. I'm going to sink the sonofa-bitch!!"

When the Bowfin finally returned to her tender she had sunk 14 Jap ships (over 1,000 tons each) and destroyed six smaller craft, totalling 70,948 tons, for a new record. Waiting on the dock for Griffith was Rear Admiral Ralph W. Christie, (then, Commander, Submarines, Southwest Pacific) with a bright Navy Cross in his hand.

Griff's second cruise on the Bowfin was another lively patrol whose first act was staged near Makassar Strait. There he contacted a large freighter escorted by a destroyer and a DE. Firing his fish in a well executed night surface attack, he scored hits on two ships, stopping the merchantman dead in her tracks and blowing up the destroyer. He waited at periscope depth until the moon came out bright and full, then finished off the freighter and sank the DE in a submerged attack, adjusting his tactics to conform with weather conditions.

Having expended 14 torpedoes in that single attack, Griffith returned to Australia to reload and started out again with Admiral Christie on board for a few thrills. Only 25 hours out he trapped a medium size unescorted freighter and successfully carried out a night torpedo attack in the Banda Sea, just north of Timor.

Action came fast and furious in those days. A day and a half later, Griffith surfaced from an early morning trim dive to face a blinker challenge by a large Japanese ship laying near the beach.

"We spent a full day getting ahead of her," said Griffith. "She was well protected by surface escorts and air patrols but that merely made her a choicer target. At first we thought she was a tanker; later we determined the ship was a seaplane tender.

"By sundown we had reached a point 17 miles ahead of the target. And there we waited until the Jap moved into a favorable position for our attack. We fired 18 torpedoes —all we had left — in spreads. Six of them hit the ship forward of the bridge, but in some miraculous manner she remained afloat. The big tender caught us in her searchlights, and splashed the sea in our vicinity with rounds of five inchers and a lot of small stuff. They drove us down deep but we got the hell out of there in one piece."

Despite her serious wounds, the Jap seaplane tender remained afloat. Later Griff found out why, when Navy intelligence identified her as the Kamoi, built in 1921 by the Sun Shipbuilding Company in Pennsylvania, with excellent compartmentation, American style. He was awarded the Silver Star for that 28 day patrol.

Griffith's next patrol also provided him and his men with more than their share of action. While prowling submerged south of Halmahera, he met a five ship convoy protected by two converted minelaying destroyers. Five land based bombers were providing air cover. Any sensible submariner would have waited until the planes left or night came. But not Walt Griffith. About 11 a.m., the Bowfin tore into two of the largest ships with three fish. The last two hit the second vessel, but the other exploded prematurely.

This made it easy for the Japs to pick up the American sub; they proceeded to bomb and depth charge her with everything in their bag of tricks. Ashcan after ashcan exploded near the submersible, breaking light-bulbs and dishes, and giving everyone a thorough shaking up.

"We waited out their attack," said Griffith. "That was all we could do. Late in the afternoon we ventured to periscope depth and sighted the damaged ship being towed by another vessel. But before we had a chance to attack again, the escort craft and planes were back on our tail with more depth charges. They were pretty smart at tracking us down."

Ashcans continued to sound off over and around the Bowfin for five additional nerve wracking hours. At last, in desperation, Griffith decided to surface and make a run to safer waters through narrow Obi Strait. As if 10 hours under attack were not sufficient, he changed his mind upon surfacing and changed course from North to South in an attempt to locate the damaged ship and sink her.

The captain couldn't find her, but he was determined to spend another night in the area. At sunrise the next morning his hunch paid off with the sighting of more Jap ships through the periscope. He saw the Nips unloading troops from a troopship; just beyond her lay the ship the Bowfin had damaged the day before. A reinforcement escort churning up the water passed the Bowfin at 500 yards, spotted the 'scope and swung around to ram.

The skipper fired a spread of two torpedoes, one of which hit the troop transport. The second was defective, as were so many in those days. He fired another spread and polished off the previous day's target, then surfaced in time to catch up with the torpedoed transport.

Now the Jap vessel had three escorts protecting her. She had been slowed down to four knots and one of the patrol craft was attempting to take her in tow. The moon came out round and dazzling, and glistened in long streaks on the placid water. Griffith had no alternative but to make a submerged attack.

"We were so close I could see the troops packed on the ship," he went on. "I let her have my last four fish but they missed, dammit, and we were driven down again by more depth charges. About 3 a.m., I decided to return to port for another load of torpedoes."

Within a week, Griff was back at the same old stand, ready for business. He didn't have to wait long before a single freighter appeared with two escorts. By racing the Bowfin ahead of the small convoy, the skipper was able to fire two spreads of four and two fish — all of which missed.

"We then survived the best goddam going over I have ever had," Griffith continued. "The Japs kept us down for six hours; our entire crew must have sweat out more than 400 pounds during the attack. I'd much rather slug it out on the surface any old time."

With deadly persistence, the Bowfin outwaited the Japs and, finally, made her way to the Philippines. Off Davao, she tracked down still another five ship convoy escorted by two fleet destroyers, and made a successful night surface attack, getting rid of seven torpedoes in 10 minutes. This time all the weapons reached their targets. Two ships went down, one was damaged.

The sub's aircraft radar soon detected an inquisitive enemy plane about five miles away. Griff speedily cleared the bridge and dove the boat to 80 feet. He had been suffering from dysentery and had just stepped into the head when a medium bomb exploded near the Bowfin and shook her sharply.

The skipper opened the door, called out, "Take her down to 120 feet," and continued to concentrate.

Another bomb exploded directly over the forward torpedo room, just a few feet from Griff's haven. Water began to drip into the compartment; some splashed into the head. Even that wasn't enough to move the old man. Again he pushed open the door.

"Let's get down to 200 feet," he ordered.

Only when he saw the amount of water in the compartment did he rush out of his retreat to check on the extent of the damage.

FIRST WAR PATROL

The Bowfin sighted her next target when she was returning from patrol with no torpedoes on board, but plenty of gun ammunition. Lookouts suddenly sighted the masts of a ship when the sub came out of a rain squall. Griffith thought she might be a patrol vessel, but there was also the possibility of her being a small coastal freighter which he might destroy by gunfire.

"I figured that if I closed to where she could see me I could find out," explained the skipper. "If she turned and ran upon sighting me then she would probably be a freighter, but if she tried to close me she would probably be a patrol vessel. Upon sighting us, the Jap ship turned and ran, so I give chase, thereby doing just what they wanted me to do. I fell neatly into the trap. They let me close slowly to gun range — all the while calling for planes."

(During the one and a half hour chase, Griff could not identify the Jap ship because her built up stern was toward him.)

At 7,800 yards, as Griffith was just about ready to shoot, the Jap ship made a full turn and fired two salvoes of five inchers that landed uncomfortably close by, and followed with a third round. At the same moment, two Petes came into sight.

The old man sounded the Klaxon twice and cried, "Dive the boat! Dive the boat! The bastards aren't playing fair."

While several depth charges popped off, Griff kicked himself for getting sucked in so easily. The "Q" ship, apparently afraid that the sub would try to torpedo her, then left the Bowfin to the planes.

"If the Jap skipper had waited five minutes before turning he and the planes could have caught me with my gun crew on deck," Griff related. "In the whole affair I played into their hands nicely — only their bungling allowed me to get away."

When the skipper surfaced later and headed for Fremantle, he sent this dispatch to Admiral Christie:

"I hereby resign from the gunshooting league."

Griffith checked his records for me to determine how many torpedoes he had fired at the Japs during his patrols on the Bowfin.

"Would you believe it?" he asked in amazement. "I have fired 101 fish valued at approximately $1,000,000. It's funny, but I've never considered their cost. War is expensive, isn't it?"

Fifty eight per cent of those torpedoes were hits. At least a dozen more would have been hits if they had not been defective. Well, that's one way to spend a million dollars and make it pay a profit.

(1) On July 16, 1944, the Bullhead felt the first caress of water when she was launched in the Thames River at Groton, Conn., by the Electric Boat Company. *INSET*: The sponsor, Mrs. Grace M. Doyle, smashing the traditional bottle of champagne against the bow of SS-332. (*Photos*: *By the Electric Boat Company*)

(2) "They slammed shut all the deck hatches . . . . In a moment, the sub began to roll gently as she neared the mouth of Apra Harbor, Guam . . . . " (*Official U. S. Navy Photo*)

ABOVE: (3) "Fifteen minutes after the close call, religious services were held in the crowded crew's quarters in the forward torpedo room . . . . James J. Brantley, the boat's yeoman and religious leader, stands with prayer book in hand." (*Official U. S. Navy Photo*) BELOW: (4) "In the crew's galley, much smaller than many apartment kitchenettes, three men prepare the chow for the boat's entire complement . . . Sometimes they perform culinary miracles here; then again, they occasionally murder meals in a most brutal manner." (*Official U. S. Navy Photo*)

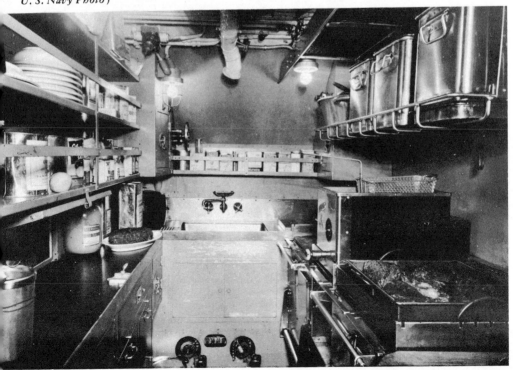

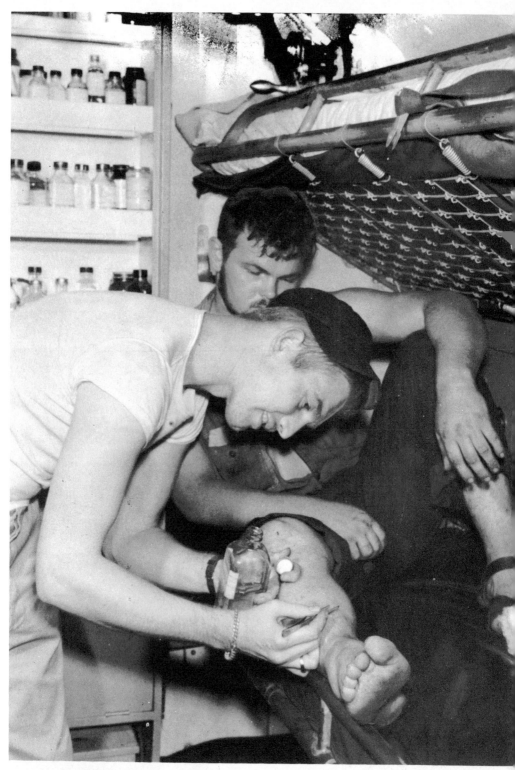

(5) "Doc" Scott removes an ingrown hair from the leg of William E. Short, torpedoman 1st class, five-year submarine veteran. (*Official U. S. Navy Photo*)

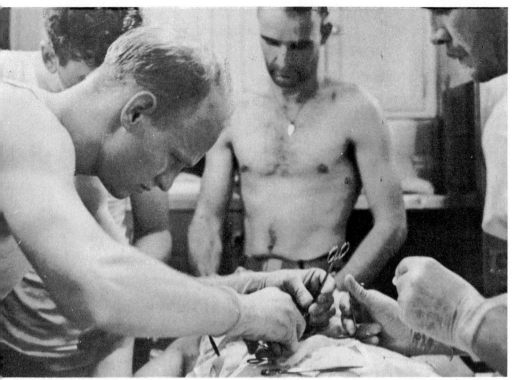

ABOVE: (6) "In the first year of war, a young pharmacist's mate, Thomas A. Moore, (left), performed a successful wardroom appendectomy on George H. Platter, fireman 1st class . . . . I wasn't particularly keen about being the guinea pig for a spring opening on the Bullhead . . ." (*Official U. S. Navy Photo*) *BELOW*: (7) "The China Coast was visible . . . . too visible . . . . through the haze. Down came the patched sails on the junks, and their skinny occupants paddled toward us with long poles." (*Photo by the author*)

ABOVE: (8) "The first survivor was carried aboard at 1:25. He was so groggy he could mutter only, 'Where's my shoes? Where's my shoes?', as if that were the most pressing problem of the moment." (*Photo by the author*) *BELOW*: (9) "Lieut. Sturm was carefully deposited in a bunk . . . . He had a pair of black eyes, a badly lacerated hand, and a swollen, bruised ankle thought to be fractured . . . . Later, he felt so well that he partook of a steak dinner." (*Official U. S. Navy Photo*)

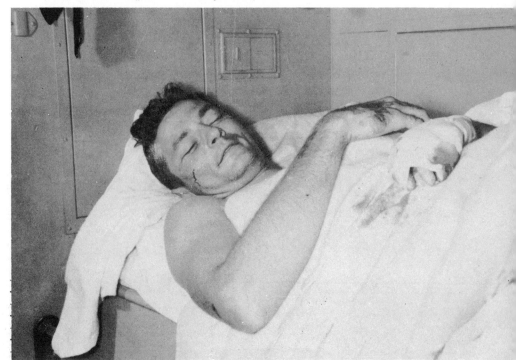

ABOVE: (10) "I experienced an indescribable thrill watching the faces of the Chinese when they spotted the big tins of meat and rice . . . . These picturesque craft are the most colorful types of boats in existence." (*Photo by the author*) BELOW: (11) "The fliers were improving rapidly, and it was noticeable in the way they ate and joked." Lieut. Charno, left, and Sgt. Tukel asked how they could transfer from the Army to the Navy, but not for submarine duty. (*Official U. S. Navy Photo*)

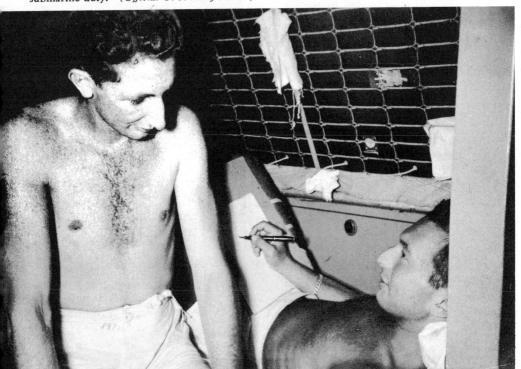

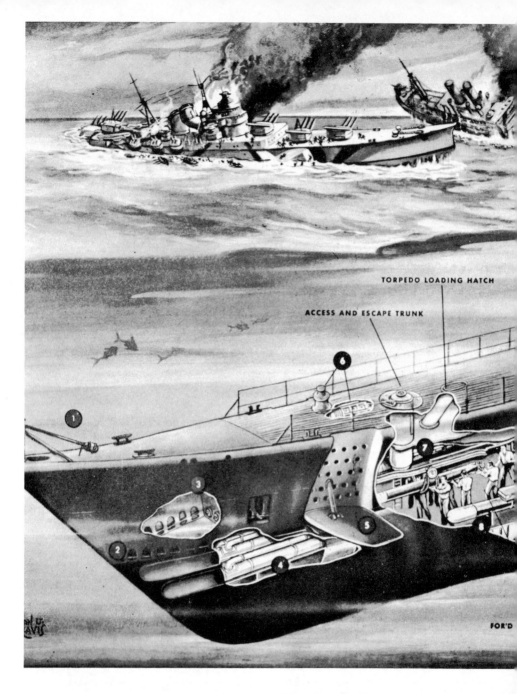

TORPEDO LOADING HATCH

ACCESS AND ESCAPE TRUNK

FOR'D

W H A T   M A K E

1. Folding bow light
2. Flood holes
3. Bow buoyancy tank
4. Torpedo tubes
5. Folding diving plane
6. Capstan, and windlass
7. Torpedo loading trolley
8. Fuel tanks and air flask

9. Torpedo room bulkhead
10. Space between inner and outer hulls serves as ballast tank
11. Storage batteries
12. Upper Control Station for surface navigation
13. Periscopes
14. Searchlight and radio direction finder
15. Radio antenna

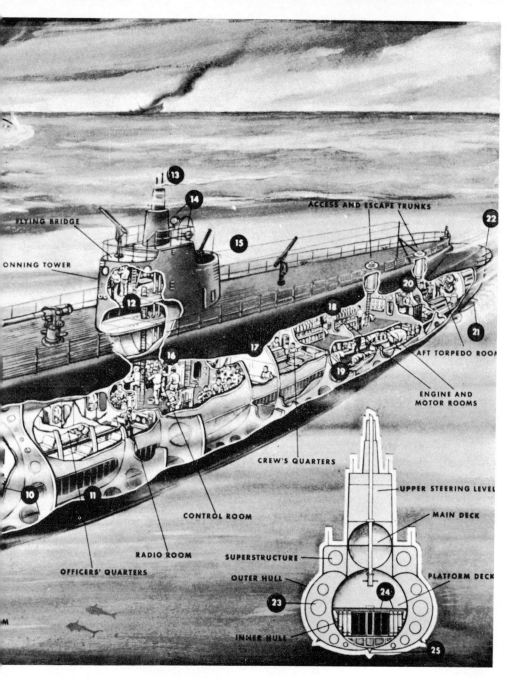

FLYING BRIDGE

CONNING TOWER

ACCESS AND ESCAPE TRUNKS

AFT TORPEDO ROOM

ENGINE AND MOTOR ROOMS

CREW'S QUARTERS

CONTROL ROOM

RADIO ROOM

OFFICERS' QUARTERS

UPPER STEERING LEVEL

MAIN DECK

SUPERSTRUCTURE

OUTER HULL

PLATFORM DECK

INNER HULL

A SUB TICK?

16. Control Room—(left to right) helmsman, navigator, skipper, "talker" who transmits commands, and diving plane operators
17. Crew's mess
18. Engine Room—Diesel engines for surface propulsion and generators for charging batteries
19. Motor Room — Electric motors, air pumps, etc. for submerged propulsion

20. Maneuvering room
21. Aft diving plane
22. Propeller guard

CROSS SECTION

23. Ballast tanks between outer and inner hulls
24. Air flasks, batteries
25. Bilge keels

(13) "The table in the wardroom was a sight to see . . . . Half of it was covered with dressings, instruments, bottles and other equipment from the first aid kit." Ens. Jack Simms II, looks over the stuff. (*Official U. S. Navy Photo*)

(14) "Men on the bridge kept a sharp lookout as we neared a Chinese junk to conduct our lend-lease operation . . . ." Note the leather sandals worn by the lookout. They were issued to all submariners to prevent fungi infections by ventilating the toes. (*Official U. S. Navy Photo*)

ABOVE: (15) "God must have known we had completed our war patrol, for He presented us with a well-nigh perfect day . . . . Comdr. Griffith put on his last suit of starched khakis and wore his scrambled egg cap for the first time as we neared Luzon." (*Official U. S. Navy Photo*)
BELOW: (16) "Several of us contributed enough clean clothes to outfit the rescued zoomies . . . Lieut. Charno was helped up the forward hatch to enjoy the fresh air." Left to right: 2nd Lieut. Charno, Lieut. Earl D. Hackman, Jr., Lieut. Pat Doherty, and Ens. Jack Simms II. (*Official U. S. Navy Photo*)

(17) It's washday and this enlisted man is busy acquiring rough, red hands while operating the submarine's washing machine. (*Official U. S. Navy Photo*)

ABOVE: (18) "Sgt. Tukel was seated topside in a chair before going aboard the gray tender with his comrades and two Fifth Air Force flight surgeons." (*Official U. S. Navy Photo*) BELOW: (19) The Bullhead's laundry is returned from the tender in half a dozen large bags. Now the crew's problem is to sort the clean, unpressed shirts and dungarees. (*Official U. S. Navy Photo*)

ABOVE: (20) This British submarine completing a war patrol is similar to the one encountered by the Bullhead during her second patrol. (*Official British Photo*) *BELOW*: (21) "During the Bullhead's second patrol in the Gulf of Siam and the Java Sea, she expended most of her ammunition sinking and damaging small Jap vessels." Here, two men are removing small arms ammunition from a magazine in preparation for an attack. (*Official U. S. Navy Photo*)

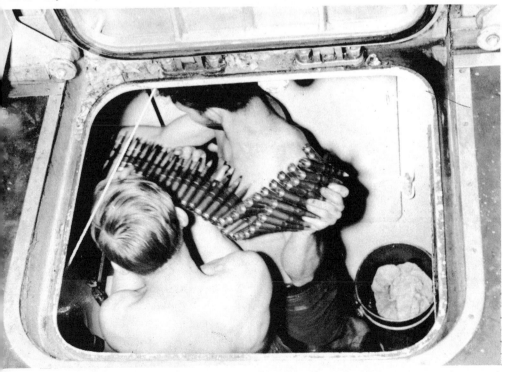

(22) Members of the refit crew load a new torpedo into the hold before the Bullhead departs on her third and final patrol. (*Official U. S. Navy Photo*)

In Fremantle, Australia, Lieut. Comdr. Edward R. Holt, Jr., reads his orders assigning him to command the USS Bullhead, as the former skipper, Comdr. Griffith, right, other officers and chiefs look on. (*Official U. S. Navy Photo*)

9

April 3 — Time again hung heavily on our hands so we scooted over to investigate a group of six Chinese fishing junks which eventually passed scrutiny. Chinese fishermen have the right idea; they take their women to sea with them. One attractive girl, wearing pajamas and a straw coolie hat, evoked mental whistles from everyone and was the subject of considerable discussion. There wouldn't have been the slightest difficulty in organizing a boarding party for that craft.

Shortly after three, a Japanese twin engine seaplane was seen several miles away and we dove. A half hour later, when the skipper took the boat to periscope depth to use the sub's eyes, he found the plane directly overhead, still hunting for us. We dove again and waited at 100 feet before resurfacing at nightfall.

April 4 — It was mighty cold in this neck of the woods, with a stiff chilly breeze whipping spray from white caps. But this is typical China Sea weather. We rolled badly in the deep swells and everyone came off watch red faced and wet.

Evidently yesterday's snooper plane was clearing the way for enemy ships that left Hong Kong sometime last night, for a dispatch informed us of a 12 ship convoy heading north about 70 miles from our position. The old man decided to go after it and ordered full speed ahead.

The combination of heavy seas and our high speed gave us a mighty uncomfortable ride, not unlike a seismic disturbance. Despite the storm, the steward's mates foolishly served thick black bean soup which didn't remain in the plates very long. Incidentally, we've been having black bean soup and dry toast daily for lunch since leaving Guam. A submarine's storage facilities are so limited that you have to eat things as they come. Bean soup was the last soup loaded so we'll be slurping it until we reach the vegetable soup section.

We gained a few miles on the Japs but the going was tough. Finally, after wallowing through turbulent seas for seven hours, our snoop planes reported that the convoy had headed close to shore where we would be unable to continue our chase.

That's the story throughout the Pacific. American cigar-shaped terrors of the sea have reaped such a magnificent harvest of choice Jap targets, that submarine warfare has become a deadly game of hide and seek. The Japs have been hiding and our subs have been hard put to find them. In recent months, the Jap fleet — or rather what is left of it — has been timorously hugging the shore by day, and anchoring in protected coves or bays at night; a repetition of our own convoy tactics off the East Coast, when German subs were destroying many poorly escorted Allied ships within sight of land.

Business for our marauders has fallen off considerably; so much so, in fact, that some submarine skippers have considered the establishment of a priority system, just in case two or more subs happen to find one Japanese ship at the same time.

Targets are so few and far between that Comdr. Griffith is continually champing at the bit for action.

"Hell, that's why I joined the submarine service," declared the skin and bones skipper. "I wanted action and now that submarine warfare is on the wane, I find it monotonous to sit around and wait day after day for a Jap ship to turn up or an American zoomie to parachute into the sea."

* * * * *

The rolling of the boat led me to have a chat with tall, blond Warner H. Scott, 24, chief pharmacist's mate, of Lowell, Mich. The chief consultant for aches and pains, our master of materia medica, is better known as "Doc," "Pill Pusher," "Quack" and a few other shipboard terms unsuitable for publication among civilians. Doc said he didn't mind most of the nicknames the boys dreamed up, but he added, "Quack cuts me to the quick."

A submarine is the only warship sailing on long patrols without a full fledged medical officer. However, pharmacist's mates have substituted commendably for them, and it's amazing how many injuries and ailments they have been able to treat successfully.

Submariners as a group are a healthy lot. In the first place, Navy medics are careful in their choice of candidates for underseas craft. Heart, lungs, ears, nose, throat, and teeth are especially checked, and men with any defects or ailments likely to recur at sea are rejected for submarine duty and assigned to surface craft which carry shipboard medics. A man's mental stability is also a deciding factor.

In the first year of the war, a 22 year old pharmacist's mate 1st class, Thomas A. Moore, of Chino Valley, Ariz., performed a wardroom appendectomy on George H. Platter, 21, fireman 1st class. (The incident was pictured in "Destination Tokyo," one of the best submarine films ever produced.) Moore's operation, assisted by an officer and two crew members, lasted four hours. (Normal time is a half hour.) A spinal anesthetic wore off and had to be supplemented with ether. Four hours later, the submarine was battling an enemy destroyer. The next morning, the patient convalesced to the breathtaking concussions from the firing of torpedoes, two depth charge attacks, two fast dives, and an aerial bombing which knocked him from the wardroom transom to the deck. Platter was performing light duties eight days after the operation.

Fortunately for everyone concerned, the operation was

a success and the man survived, but immediately afterward the Navy Bureau of Medicine issued an inflexible directive banning appendectomies aboard submarines.

I was particularly interested since my appendix had kicked up just before sailing in February with a fast carrier task force for the first Navy plane strikes against the Japanese home islands. I had gone aboard a Navy hospital ship at Ulithi Atoll for an examination and was told by a four striper that my worm wasn't quite ready for removal*.

I wasn't keen about being the guinea pig for a spring opening on a submarine. Doc Scott assured me he wouldn't try an appendectomy under any circumstances, but would freeze an acute case until the patrol was completed. That set my mind at ease.

There isn't room for a sick bay — as such — aboard a sub. If a man is ill enough, Doc keeps him in his bunk. He has a couple of lockers filled with bottles, books, bandages, jars, and instruments; they are in the crowded crew's quarters in the after compartment where he treats his patients. Doc doesn't maintain regular hours for sick call, but prescribes at any time, day or night, when he isn't on watch. In addition to his medical duties, he also stands sound and periscope watches and holds regular inspections of galleys, living areas and sanitation facilities for cleanliness.

"Most of my cases are colds and earaches caused by the air conditioning system and air pressure," Scott explained, as we sat on the edge of his bunk. "Constipation is widespread because of the limitations of our diet, with another contributing factor the lack of exercise. Then there are the usual minor ailments such as stomach aches, sore throats, burns, ingrown nails and hair, ringworm, and infections of cuts. The infections are caused by the men failing to report minor

*A former Navy doctor, Wesley M. Wright, removed the author's appendix in Hollywood on March 25, 1946, nearly a year later.

injuries and have them cleaned and dressed. Knock on wood, they haven't come up yet with anything I haven't been able to handle. I can also perform emergency dental work, and insert temporary fillings. Extractions? I never touch them."

Doc reported that he is plagued with many cases of seasickness when new men join the boat. But there isn't much he can do for them except try the psychological treatment of giving the sufferers a couple of aspirin.

"Many men aboard a sub do not have enough work to keep their minds occupied," said Doc. "Consequently, they have too much time to think and imagine things. They imagine they have a pain here, an ache there, and the first thing you know they BELIEVE they are really sick. Then they come to me with their story. I always make it a point to give these hypochondriacs a pill — even though it's only sodium bicarb or aspirin. They imagine they're taking some complicated medicine and soon feel well again. I used to think only women bothered doctors with imaginary ailments. Brother, some submariners are in a class by themselves."

Even Comdr. Griffith has been under Doc Scott's care. On two occasions at night, he has sped from his cabin into the dimly lit passageway — rigged for red — and fallen several feet down the open battery well outside his quarters; this is open when someone neglects to put the metal guard in place while checking gravity in the huge cells. The skipper's injuries were painful lacerations and cuts. Doc's treatment included dressings and a warning to take it easy.

At her commissioning, the Bullhead was issued 157 different medical items, including penicillin and a voluminous manual. Doc estimates the whole kit's value as $300. His pride and joy is a new otoscope, for examining ears, which he wangled for himself before leaving the States. One of his own innovations is the adaptation of an ordinary nose atomizer for spraying sulfa powder evenly on open wounds.

There's a sun lamp aboard, but few men use it; it's hidden somewhere aft. The attitude of most submariners toward sunbathing is summed up tersely in what one man told me.

"Cripes, if I had wanted to sun myself," he asserted, "I'd have asked for duty on an aircraft carrier!"

Multiple vitamin capsules are on the tables at meal time to aid night vision and offset the deficiency of sunshine. Meals tend to be too starchy, in my opinion. Submarine chow costs about 93 cents a day, considerably higher than on surface craft.

The Bullhead's seagoing medical library consists of: Medical Compend, a summary of symptoms and their treatment; Naval Hygiene; Minor Surgery; Treatment in General Practice (Doc Scott calls this a "wonderful book"); the Hospital Corps Handbook — 1939; Manual of the Medical Department and a number of monthly and quarterly publications distributed by the Bureau of Medicine.

Before donning Navy blues and whites five and a half years ago, Doc said he was a jack-of-all-trades. He signed up for the hospital course at the Norfolk, Va., Naval Hospital, studied Chemistry, Hygiene and Sanitation, Nursing and Ward Management, Materia Medica and Therapeutics, First Aid and Minor Surgery, Anatomy and Physiology, Diets and Messing. Meeting his wife in Norfolk, he said, was the only favorable comment he could make about that city.

Scott made several war patrols on an old S-boat in the Aleutians, operating out of Dutch Harbor and Attu on runs to Paramushiro. On the third day of his second trip, a machinist's mate tightening bolts near the crankshaft slipped on some oil and lost four toes in the shaft. Doc zipped out his kit, stopped the bleeding, deftly took eight sutures and treated the man for shock.

When the sub returned to her base the patient was up and around, apparently none the worse for his accident.

Doc's shore hobby was building furniture and, after the war, he plans to return to Michigan to become an interior decorator.

"My medical experience will come in handy," he pointed out. "At least I'll know how to treat my thumb when I pound it with a hammer."

*　*　*　*　*

Regarding the health conditions and habitability aboard submarines, Lieut. Comdr. William S. Francis, (MC), USN, has made the following observations in the Hospital Corps Quarterly:

War patrols of over 55 days are not conducive to maximum efficiency . . . . Long dives of 16 to 18 hours result in headaches for most men and cause them to think and act slowly . . . The most appreciated man aboard is a good baker . . . Instances of food poisoning have been surprisingly low . . . Many men, after their first experience at being depth charged, become "nervous," often get nauseated and develop diarrhea.

Instances of hysteria or war neurosis have been at a minimum . . . The best morale booster, according to one submarine commander, is the sound of one's own torpedo exploding in the vitals of an enemy ship. He compared undergoing a depth charge attack following a successful torpedoing, to a woman going through her first pregnancy; it is painful going through it, but when it's over, you are proud of your baby!

10

Sunday, April 8 — It started out to be a peaceful Sunday despite the foul weather topside and deep swells that soaked the men on the bridge. Damp clouds practically rested on the crests of the whitecaps as the Bullhead, minding her own business, plowed through the South China Sea.

Below deck some men lay in their bunks and snoozed; others were reading or chewing the fat. I had closed myself in the tiny yeoman's office and was engrossed in the armed forces paper covered edition of a book titled "Thunder Mountain." I was midway through a chapter describing log-rolling claps of thunder reverberating on an inaccessible precipice.

Suddenly IT happened, as though sound effects were being synchronized with my reading. I was jarred by a series of three loud bursts. I knew something was happening when the Klaxon sounded three times even though we were on surface. (Three honks signal to surface, two designate a dive.)

An excited voice screamed, "Dive the boat!! Dive the boat!!!"

And dive the boat, they did. As sea water flowed into the wide open valves of our tanks, the Bullhead was shaken by the concussions from three nearby explosions. Gobs of dust and fuzz fluttered from the small electric fan on the bulkhead onto my book.

Though the boat dove rapidly, it didn't seem half fast enough. Then, as she leveled off, we heard three more explosions, not as close as the first. Crewmen jammed the control room to ask a thousand questions.

"Everything happened so damned fast I could hardly believe we were being attacked," explained Ray Strassle, who had been on the bridge when everything began. "I was conning the horizon when a lookout yelled. I turned around, and he pointed at a four engine plane with double rudder that had popped out from behind thick clouds astern of us. We identified the plane as a probable Liberator (B-24).

"The fly-fly boy was flying low, between 1,000 and 1,500 feet, and knew damn well where he was going," Strassle went on. "We didn't have time to get an IFF (identification signal from a friendly plane) from him. Only a few seconds elapsed from the time we sighted the bomber till the lousy bastard made an instrument run on us and dropped that first string of bombs. I was so excited that, subconsciously, I pressed the diving alarm three times, probably because of the three bombs."

"Fred Jewell was so spellbound by the attack that he just stood openfaced at his lookout post and watched the eggs drop; I had to yank him off the platform and push him down the ladder. The plane crossed our starboard quarter and I saw the eggs splash into the sea about 75 yards astern of us. Whew!"

Men in the maneuvering and after torpedo rooms were shaken up a bit by the underwater blasts. Scores of fuses rolled around the deck and a small trickle of water dripped through a relief valve that had been broken on a water circulating line. Dust fell from countless nooks and crannies. One serious case of constipation was known to be cured by the attack. The small nickel slot machine went out of commission for the duration of the patrol, but the Bullhead was otherwise undamaged.

A few minutes after Strassle finished his story there came the pinging sounds of strafing slugs plunking into the water still farther away. Needless to say, we remained submerged all afternoon.

Comdr. Griffith immediately drafted an indignant dispatch to headquarters, complaining of the bombing by a probable Liberator. He requested an investigation of reports by Fifth Air Force planes patrolling in our area, which is designated as a safety zone where NO submarines are to be attacked.

At divine services two hours later, a capacity crowd of sober submariners jammed the forward torpedo room "chapel." Ray Strassle read the Call to Worship. One of the lookouts during the attack, big, blond, bearded John L. Hancock, gunner's mate 2nd class, of Orange, Calif., read a prayer. This is his first patrol.

We sang Hymn 59, "What a Friend We Have in Jesus," then Billy Ireland delivered the Lesson, "Courage Versus Fear." Billy, a torpedoman from Stonington, Conn., is one of the most serious men on the boat. The service ended with the singing of the timely Hymn, "He Leadeth Me."

April 9 — We haven't sunk any enemy ships yet, but we have certainly been busy dodging Japanese mines, steering clear of Chinese junks, keeping away from our own warships, remaining out of sight of possible targets, and diving once or twice daily because of snooping search planes, both Japanese and American.

Today, two zoomies definitely identified as Japanese drove us down twice within two hours, but they didn't drop any bombs. That fact has been surprising throughout the patrol; we have submerged at least 20 times for enemy planes and they've never bombed or strafed us. We're not complaining, of course. Merely reflecting.

April 10 — The Bullhead was submerged about 14 hours. As yet, ComSubPac hasn't sent us any assignment and we haven't had any customers for our lifeguard service. But we're still hopeful.

April 11 — We were underwater for another long stretch of 13 hours. The Wednesday matinee (smoking permitted in all parts of the theater) featured a western picture, "King of the Cowboys," with Roy

Rogers and his palomino. Oh well, the film helped to pass the hours.

April 12 — Another long dive of 13 hours. Everyone's eyes began to feel uncomfortable from the worn-out air. I had trouble lighting my pipe; the matches just wouldn't stay lit because the oxygen supply was getting low.

At two a.m., after surfacing, we picked up a contact. In rapid succession, someone at the aircraft radar reported a plane only 500 yards away; Keith Phillips yelled, "Left full rudder!", and the skipper cried, "Dive the boat!"

A half hour later we resurfaced in time to see a big four engine seaplane cross our bow. Earl Hackman, the OD, speedily pulled in his neck and dove again. After breakfast, the Bullhead surfaced for the third time, and the skipper went topside with his carbine to sink an oil drum seen floating nearby. He thought it might have served at some time as a mine buoy.

April 13 (East Longitude Date) — On surface all day. At 11 o'clock, we heard the startling announcement of President Roosevelt's sudden death. The news came as a shock to everyone.

Radiomen got the first flash over the submarine circuit from Guam. I heard the report direct from Radio Tokyo. Against the somber musical background of "When Day is Done," played on a tinny piano, an English-speaking announcer emoted with commiseration for the American people. The Jap eulogized Mr. Roosevelt and his achievements. We could hardly believe our ears.

I couldn't help recalling how exhausted FDR seemed at the 1944 Hawaii conference with Admiral Nimitz and General MacArthur; how dark the circles were under his eyes, and how deep the wrinkles in his face. He appeared old and very tired. Correspondents were requested by Elmer Davis not to watch the President being carried from the interior of the home where he was staying, to the spacious lawn overlooking Waikiki. When we were finally told to turn around, we noticed how his hands shook as he lit a cigarette. He had considerable difficulty in hearing our questions.

At regular intervals throughout the day, the Japanese radio presented additional details about the President's death. Reception from the States was badly jumbled because of poor atmospheric conditions somewhere along the route, and we could not pick up a complete broadcast concerning the Commander in Chief for many hours.

The Bullhead's radio is our only contact with the outside world. We can pick up Tokyo, Shanghai, Saigon, Chungking and also short wave programs beamed from San Francisco to the Philippines. Reception is unsatisfactory nine times out of 10 because of annoying whistling, static, scratching, and garbling. Our usual fare, Oriental music, with its monotonous sing-songy vocalists from unidentifiable Asiatic stations, is entertaining only up to a point.

Most entertaining of all are the amusing Japanese commentators who spout in English from Radio Tokyo. They are always good for a hearty laugh as they read their nonsensical propaganda. Today, one wag described the United States Navy as "losing 300 warships off Okinawa."

"The Fifth Fleet," he added, "managed to escape annihilation only by the grace of a storm. Imperial forces have destroyed 11 battleships, 13 cruisers, 45 destroyers and many other large warships."

What, no PT boats or submarines? If we had suffered all the huge losses claimed by the Japs, it is a certainty that the Pacific war would have become a stalemate or ended in defeat for the United States.

Another commentator, crudely distorting the facts,

announced that the United States Marines on Okinawa had gained 200 yards in 24 hours.

"Do you realize what a small gain that is?" the buffoon asked sarcastically. "A football field is 100 yards long, and twice that length was the infinitesimal distance over-run yesterday by the mighty Marines. Hah!

"Why, the world's record for the 200 meter dash is only 20.7 seconds, yet it took the highly vaunted Leather-necks 24 hours to cover the same distance. Ho, ho, ho, my friends, they have chosen a hard nut to crack this time. The gallant Japanese defenders and the superior Japanese Air Force (superior only in suffering losses) will make life even more uncomfortable for the United States Marines."

Nearly every day the Japs also extolled their special attack Kamikaze corps, mentioning with reverence the names and addresses of a few of its fanatical pilots who went out to die — and did.

Our reply to Radio Tokyo was, "Pure, unadulterated BUNK!"

* * * * *

This is Friday the 13th, and an unlucky day for an American fighter pilot reported shot down this morning somewhere near Hong Kong Harbor. The skipper checked his charts for the position and shook his head sadly.

"Much as I'd like to try to pick up the fly-fly boy," he said, "we'd be crazy to risk it."

A later report informed us the pilot was waiting patiently in a rubber boat for a PBM rescue plane being sent to the scene to attempt a water landing, pick up the airman, and take off again under the very noses of the Japs. We hoped they made it but never did find out.

* * * * *

The Bullhead continued to pound through heavy seas, making life unpleasant for everyone. Finally, we dove for some peace and quiet, and the captain passed the welcome word for movies. One scene in the film showed coeds changing from street clothes to pajamas, and the audience cheered so vociferously that the projectionist had to stop the machine, reverse the film, and run it through three times before the commotion subsided. And all that they saw was a flash of white shoulder and a hand rolling down a nylon stocking — or reasonable facsimile thereof — on a shapely limb. A scene that passed the movie censors' office without a deletion.

April 14 — Comdr. Griffith took the sub to 400 feet for a test. The outside pressure on every square inch of our double-skinned hull was over 170 pounds, but nothing happened. We ate breakfast 100 feet below the surface, where three minute eggs are prepared in one minute, and the barometer always reads inches higher than it does in the open. No activity off Hong Kong, so the skipper authorized showers and a movie. The feature was "You Can't Escape Forever."

Sunday, April 15 — I went topside for the first time in seven days. It seems that something always happens to us on Sunday, or whenever I climb on deck. Three weeks ago, two planes drove us down twice during the afternoon. Last week, we were attacked by the four engine bomber thought to be an American B-24.

Shortly after lunch today, lookouts sighted another floating mine. This one had longer horns, although it was smaller than the job we detonated a few days ago. The skipper called out the 20-millimeter gun crew to destroy it. Although they plugged enough holes in the steel case to sink it, it didn't explode.

The Bullhead rendezvoused with the Tigrone for a few minutes and swapped information. Later in the afternoon, one of our search planes reported a Jap gunboat skirting the coast of Hainan Island. Griff decided to try to intercept her by revving up all engines to full speed.

During the Sunday religious services, we suddenly felt the Bullhead swerve sharply to starboard, then to port. The captain raised his eyebrows questioningly and looked up with an anxious frown. Then a quartermaster broke through the crowd and interrupted the services with, "There's something going on, captain. The OD just called, 'Right full rudder' and 'Left full rudder.' "

With that announcement, the old man swept past me to go topside. Meanwhile, John Hancock continued with his sermon on, "The Love for God." In a few minutes Griffith returned and everyone looked relieved. As he passed me he whispered, "Another mine, but we haven't time to bother with it now."

When he recovered his breath, he delivered a memorial address in memory of the late President.

"As we all know, the Navy was President Roosevelt's favorite branch of the armed forces, and the Navy Hymn was his favorite hymn," the captain concluded. "Therefore, it is fitting that we sing this Hymn, 'Eternal Father, Strong to Save,' in memory of him."

11

Monday, April 16 — The skipper played a long shot today and won. He stuck his head right down the lion's throat and emerged with three badly hurt Army fliers from a B-25 crew.

Taking the Bullhead into a blind bombing zone, where our planes were free to attack any submarines they saw, Comdr. Griffith sped to within four miles of the China Coast, into a heavily mined area with only 12 fathoms of water — sufficient for submerging but not enough to hide us if we were trapped by the Japs. There he supervised the transfer on board of the American airmen, who had been rescued first by Chinese junks after they had ditched their burning plane in the sea.

The three fliers were survivors of a crew of six. We found them two hours after they had gone down, just as the junks were leaving the burning wreckage. An hour later, the Bullhead's mission might have been unsuccessful, since there were more than a score of junks widely scattered about these perilous waters, and we would have had to look over each one to locate the survivors. That would have been a highly dangerous business, what with Jap airfields in the area, and scores of explosive charges hiding beneath the surface.

First news of the downed Mitchell bomber from the 71st Tactical Reconnaissance Group arrived at 11:20 a.m., as we were patrolling our lifeguard station. An urgent message came in on the lifeguard frequency for Birddog, our code name, with the terse information, "Plane down with two survivors," and their position.

Keith Phillips, our navigator, went to work with his

pencil and instruments, and fixed the given position as only 35 miles from us in Bias Bay, midway between Hong Kong and Swatow. He plotted a course to the spot, and we started out at full speed.

Griffith looked at his charts for a while, and said to me, "The way I figure it, those zoomies ought to be able to wade ashore. There's about 12 fathoms of water in that area, but that doesn't help us. The Japs could easily spot us."

A couple of planes from the Philippines covered us for a while, but they ran short of fuel and had to leave. Meanwhile, the radio shack decoded another message, informing us that some P-38's were covering the downed plane. And a PV Ventura was on its way to protect us.

The skipper nibbled hurriedly through lunch and returned to the bridge. After the departure of our air cover, his face took on a glum expression. He called for Lieut. (jg) Donald Henriksen, our communications officer.

"We're going inside the 100 fathom curve, Don," said Griff. "You'd better destroy our decoding equipment and other secret gear."

The men went work with sledge hammers. They pounded away at reels and instruments valued at approximately $10,000. Finally, they nonchalantly heaved the wreckage overboard.

The fly-fly boys couldn't have chosen a more propitious day for their dunking. The sea was smooth, visibility excellent; the day was sunny and warm. And best of all, the Bullhead was cruising not too far from the accident.

At one o'clock, an arch of black smoke hove into sight and the captain poured on the heat — all engines at flank speed, our maximum. Patiently waiting on the bridge, with his moving picture camera and color film, was the Navy photographer, Steve Birch. I was delegated to help out by shooting still photographs with his 4x5 Speed Graphic.

The smoke hung motionless in the sky as we came nearer and nearer, past a fleet of multi-sized junks, which we devoutly hoped were Chinese.

Then the Ventura appeared overhead and we felt reassured, even though he could stick with us only 20 minutes. That was better than nothing, of course, but I never could figure out why operations did not send out a plane with a greater range. In the distance now, we saw two tiny junks perhaps a half mile from the smoke, still billowing from the burning wreckage. Griffith asked the Ventura pilot to investigate. He swooped down low over the water and reported that the injured men might be on the craft. As he spoke, both junks hoisted signals in the shape of straw baskets atop short masts at their sterns.

The China Coast was visible . . . too visible . . . through the haze. In sight was the shoreline with its good earth, trees, brownish patches of cultivated land and, beyond, barren mountains. I turned my field glasses on the junks, now less than a mile away, and could distinguish one of the survivors, a tall man in khaki leaning again a mast.

We came closer. The captain called out, "All stop, left full rudder." Then "Right full rudder." The roar of the Diesels faded away and the only sound was that of the Bullhead sliding through the water. Down came the patched sails on the junks, and their skinny occupants paddled toward us with long poles. Although the face of the man in khaki coveralls was smeared with blood and swollen grotesquely from his injuries, I am certain I saw a faint smile on his lips as he waved weakly to us.

The rescue party piled on deck with a Jacob's ladder, lines, stretchers, and other equipment. Griffith was signalling the junks to pull alongside, but the Chinese didn't understand. They just chattered like monkeys and gesticulated wildly.

Finally, they caught on, and the two decrepit craft came alongside and took our lines. But our bow was a few feet too high for easy access, so there was a several second delay while Pat Doherty flooded the forward tanks and lowered us five or six feet. It was 1:25 when the first survivor was carried aboard. He was the tall flier whom I had seen standing.

He was so groggy, he could mutter only, "Where's my shoes? Where's my shoes?", as if that were the most pressing problem of the moment.

The Chinese on the other junk lifted a pile of rags and matting from the deck, uncovering a second survivor; then to our surprise, a third. We had expected only two.

There were nine Chinese in one of the weatherbeaten junks, seven in the other. All appeared to be undernourished and wore ragged shorts and coolie hats or, in a few cases, filthy, misshapen felt hats. In their faces, and in their patched, tattered sails, were reflected China's plight — a poverty-stricken people in a long suffering nation ripped asunder by greed, civil war, floods, and pestilence.

They could speak to us only with gestures and went through the motions of eating and rubbing their stomachs. But they beamed in appreciation when our men handed them several cartons of cigarettes, fresh bread, frozen chicken, luncheon meat (Spam), matches, blankets, and a five gallon can filled with rice.

The Ventura that had planned to cover us for only 20 minutes was still circling overhead. The pilot said he was so thrilled at watching the rescue that he had forgotten about his dwindling fuel supply. He said he was leaving for his base immediately, before we had to perform another rescue — of him. We waved our fervent thanks, and he disappeared over the horizon as we were streaking toward the open sea with full power.

Two fliers were placed in lower bunks in the four man officers' stateroom occupied by Earl Hackman, Eldridge Erickson, Paul Gossett, and Ray Strassle. The third man was carefully deposited in a bunk in the chiefs' quarters. All were in shock and trembling. They complained of feeling cold, so we piled blankets over them.

It was a providential day for New York City, especially Brooklyn and Richmond Boroughs. The three lucky men lived in the big city, within 12 miles of one another. They were:

2nd Lieut. Irving Charno, 22, pilot of the B-25, of Brooklyn; 2nd Lieut. Harold V. Sturm, 23, co-pilot, of Richmond Hill, and Sgt. Robert Tukel, 23, radioman and waist gunner, also of Brooklyn.

Not so fortunate as this trio were their fellow crewmen killed in the crash landing: 2nd Lieut. Harry Cohen, navigator, of Norfolk, Va.; Sgt. James Pasledni, engineer, of Bellaire, Ohio, and Sgt. John J. White, tail gunner, of Philadelphia, Pa.

Charno, a gangling lad with curly hair, was cut and bruised about the eyes and mouth, and had an ugly gash in his leg. Sturm had a pair of black eyes, a badly lacerated hand, and a swollen, bruised ankle thought by Doc Scott to be fractured. Tukel suffered two deep, four inch lacerations on his scalp, lacerations on his legs and body, and severe pains in his chest and back.

Doc Scott, aided by James F. Collins, fireman 1st class, of Syracuse, N. Y., and William J. Ralston, Jr., seaman 1st class, of San Bernardino, Calif., cut off the men's clothing and went to work on their injuries. An officer placed their few remaining personal possessions in envelopes and sealed them.

(The Chinese fishermen had taken two wrist watches, a ring, shoes, and the contents of the fliers' billfolds. Later they applied to the American consuls in Hong

Kong, Kowloon, and Chungking for a reward. Their letter follows:

> 345 Nathan Rd.,
> c/o Woo Ping Hotel
> Kowloon — Dec. 21, 1945

Dear Sir:

I wish to bring to your notice the following occurence and hope that you will be able to answer our appeal. On the 5th of March, 1945 [incorrect date], at 12 o'clock, I was fishing in Bias Bay when nine (9) Allied bombers appeared and attacked the Japanese occupied area of Ping Hai. One of the planes unfortunately crashed into the sea some considerable distance from my boat. Without delay I and my eight companions proceeded to the spot and were able to rescue two of the airmen, who were injured, and escort them back to their submarine. From the submarine we received gifts — one sword, a rifle and two hand watches — but unfortunately on our return voyage to our port, we were attacked by armed pirates and robbed. The only proof we have of this happening is a medal given to us by one of the wounded pilots. Owing to our present position, we are appealing to you, sir, to find us employment or reimburse us in some manner.

We would greatly appreciate an early reply to this letter.

I am, Your Obedient Servants,

/s/ CAPTAIN SO HEE
/s/ SEAMAN LEE FAT LO

One consul wrote Sgt. Tukel in January 1946, that he could have settled the claim for $15, but he did not have the funds or the authorization, or proof that the story was true. Upon requesting evidence from the Chinese, the official was given a document which he then forwarded to Tukel. The gunner said it was his identification folder lifted from his billfold by his rescuers.)

Comdr. Griffith broke out a box of 12 small bottles of Lejon brandy, thereby designating a singular event. The injured men finished a total of three bottles; the remaining nine disappeared during the excitement.

OVERDUE AND PRESUMED LOST

I administered surettes of morphine to Charno and Tukel, to allay their pain. Then I dug up a fresh cake of Ivory soap for Paul Gossett to use in lathering Tukel's scalp, before shaving it with his straight razor — the only one on the Bullhead. Scott later took more than 20 sutures in the gunner's wounds, sprinkled sulfa powder on them, and covered his head with a turban-like dressing.

Someone washed the dried blood from Charno's face and he began to look more presentable. Doc patched him up, then turned to Sturm's mutilated hand. He didn't take any stitches in it, but sprinkled sulfa powder on the limb and covered it with a loose dressing. By sundown, Sturm felt so well that he partook of a steak dinner and seemed to be enjoying his submarine cruise. The others were unable to keep water or fruit juice on their stomach.

It was Sturm, a former teller with the National City Bank of New York, who first told us their story.

"We left our Fifth Air Force base at San Marcellino Airdrome, Luzon, this morning in The Klunk with four other B-25's, two squadrons of P-38's and some Navy planes to attack Jap shipping along the China Coast," he said. "We rendezvoused at Pratas with the fighters and began our sweep. North of Hong Kong, we sighted more than 30 junks loaded with military equipment, and all of us went in abreast for a low level bombing and strafing attack. We made the run just over their decks, perhaps 25 to 50 feet above them, and didn't notice any ack-ack.

"I don't know what happened then," he continued. "Tukel said he felt a concussion under his feet; when he looked out he saw our port engine smoking badly. Soon it began to blaze. Our automatic fire-fighting equipment had conked out, and we really began to worry when the needles in the gas gauges dropped steadily toward 'empty'. Could be that one of our own

500 pound bombs — or one from another plane with us — skipped and bounced from the sea, hitting our plane between the fuselage and the port engine, destroying the hydraulic and fuel systems*.

"Charno was at the controls," Sturm went on. "We hastily decided to ditch The Klunk before the flames reached the fuel tanks. We were down to 1,000 feet and losing power every second when the port landing gear dropped down. The plane hit the water hard, nosed in and filled quickly. By this time, we were about 30 miles from the targets. All the plexiglass had shattered and cut Charno and me. Flames spread through the plane. We struggled to escape through an open hatch, and after we got out, noticed Tukel in a daze near the plane's elevators. We called to the others but didn't see them. Another plane in our formation dropped a rubber life raft, but we lacked the strength to reach it. We just floated around helplessly in our inflated Mae Wests.

"Those Chinese junks paddled alongside about an hour later," he said. "One picked up Charno; the other pulled Tukel and me aboard. The Chinese kept jabbering away, but we couldn't understand a word they said. But whenever they heard a plane approaching, they covered us with nets, straw mats, and large coolie hats, just in case it might be the Japs. One fisherman removed my shoes. Tukel had already kicked off his in the water, and removed his pants.

---

*When the injured fliers returned to their base, they learned that their plane probably had been struck by 40-millimeter gunfire. 1st Lieut. Frederick Kluth, another Fifth Air Force pilot, reported having his nose door shot off by 40-millimeter gunfire in the same run with Charno. It was Kluth who tossed his life raft to the injured men after they crashed. In doing so, the raft struck an elevator of his plane and damaged it. A squadron of P-38's then covered Charno's wrecked plane for a while and sent the urgent message to the Bullhead. Kluth was awarded the Bronze Star for his aid to the B-25 survivors. He was shot down two weeks later in a raid over Luzon. One of his crew escaped with the help of guerillas and reported that Kluth and the others had died from severe burns.

"I can't remember how long we lay on deck until a Chinese shook me and pointed seaward to an approaching boat. At first, we were afraid she was Japanese, and those black bearded faces of the crew frightened us. Then I saw the red haired man (Griffith) on the bridge and I knew he must be an American, because I had never heard of a red haired Jap.

"Next, I saw the Stars and Stripes fluttering from the mast. A lump piled up in my throat; I felt like crying but couldn't start the tears aflowing. It was like sailing past the Statue of Liberty after being overseas five years, or listening to a band play 'Over There,' at a Fifth Avenue parade. God, it was a wonderful feeling to see the sub!"

Tukel, a former clerk, said he didn't have time to fasten his safety belt before the crash, and attributed his battering to that fact. He escaped through the starboard waist hatch, got his Mae West inflated after a difficult time, but couldn't make the 100 yards to the empty raft.

"On 35 of our 37 missions I had worn my lucky green cap," he said. "Two trips ago, it disappeared, and then this happened. Maybe there's a connection."

Three crewmen, Scott, Collins, and Ralston, stood four hour watches as "nurses" during the night. Nearly everyone on board has poked his head through the green curtain to say "Hello," to the fly-fly boys and inquire about their condition.

The table in the wardroom was a sight to see after dinner; half of it was covered with bandages, instruments, bottles, and tubes from Doc Scott's first aid kit. Clothes lay all over the place, and two men slept soundly in the bunks, while Pat Doherty and Don Henriksen battled over a game of acey-ducey.

There was no griping tonight about the boredom and monotony of submarine patrols. All our cruising and patient waiting during the past several weeks have been more than compensated by the rescue of these three men, even though they are from Brooklyn.

The fact remains that Comdr. Griffith did not have to go into the blind bombing zone; it was entirely at his discretion to proceed so close to shore in such shallow water. He could have reported the rescue mission impracticable for a submarine, and gone on his way. Instead, he felt a moral obligation toward his fellow servicemen, and went ahead with the job despite its dangers.

The skipper's comment on the day's work was made when he came down from the bridge at midnight.

"Wonder why I feel as if I had been through a clothes wringer," he sighed, and sank weakly into a wardroom chair.

The two officers deprived of their bunks moved into warm sacks just vacated by two others going on watch. I sacked in above Charno in the small cabin across the passageway.

12

April 17 — Last night, the skipper headed toward Subic Bay and sent a dispatch to ComSubPac, telling of the rescue, and listing the trio's names. A duplicate message was sent to Fifth Air Force headquarters to enable personnel officers there to start the machinery turning for the notification of next of kin of the dead and injured.

The three lucky guys from Brooklyn passed a restless night, but that was to be expected. As if their crash and injuries did not provide sufficient grist for their mental mills, the young zoomies were also worried about being on board a submarine.

"Cripes," one said, "we've jumped from the frying pan right into the fire."

I tried to point out to them how fortunate they were to be on the Bullhead, the only submarine in the Pacific with a correspondent on board.

"And there's no extra charge for this personal service," I added.

They complained during the day that every muscle and bone in their bodies ached and throbbed from the shock of their crash landing. Consequently, they were scarcely in a frame of mind to be at ease when they heard gunfire after evening chow.

Another mine had been sighted at 6 p.m., this time a real old one that persistently refused to explode after scores of rounds of ammunition had been fired at it. Pierced at last by several shells, the rusty outer case finally filled with water and the mine reluctantly sank.

April 18 — Admiral Lockwood ordered the Bullhead to complete her patrol, unless the condition of any injured man required immediate hospitalization. The fliers felt much better, so Griff decided to turn back to the China Coast. My hopes for a speedy end to this cruise have been shattered.

We were patrolling tonight just off the South China Coast. If the wind were blowing strong enough from the proper direction, we would be able to inhale those tantalizing aromas from chow mein and egg foo yong being prepared in better class restaurants ashore in Canton and Hong Kong. The impoverished masses, however, subsist on a meager diet of boiled rice and fish.

This is the region that has given the United States so many of its Chinese residents. Nine out of 10 Chinese in America were born in the Canton area or descended from progenitors born there.

I'll wager that many a Chinese-American would give anything to trade places with me today to catch a glimpse of his war torn homeland. It's the principal aim of practically every Chinese, either to die in China or have his remains buried there after death.

In Cuba two years ago, I visited Havana's unusual Chinese cemetery where the graves are emptied at the end of three years and the remains tossed into an open air heap, unless provisions had been made for their transfer to China.

One small building was piled high with hundreds of small boxes, each about the size of a case of whisky, duly labeled in Chinese, and sealed. Each contained the remains of a Chinese who had died and left instructions and funds to send his bones back to China for final interment. They were awaiting the resumption of shipping to the Far East.

Enemy planes forced the Bullhead down twice, and the first sounds of the Klaxon diving alarm made our airmen-guests tremble as if in shock. The frightening sound grates in my ears too, even though I have heard it many times.

One of the aircraft appeared from out of nowhere

with all his running lights on — definitely an infrequent occurrence in enemy territory. It must have been an accident.

April 19 — We have had word of the mass movement of a B-29 bombardment wing from China to the Marianas. Let's hope the Superfortresses stick to their flying, without violating orders not to molest submarines.

There was no rest for the weary. Planes continued to appear during the day and we were forced to submerge three times. The second time, at 8 p.m., a Jap float plane made a deliberate run on us, swung around as we dove, and released two depth charges that exploded a few hundred yards away. The skipper spoke dryly of this inimical act.

"It destroys my faith in mankind," he said with disgust. "Goddammit, we have been minding our own business without bothering anybody out here. The Japs shouldn't be so difficult to get along with."

The fliers, when they heard the loud underwater explosions, easily distinguishable from bombs by their more solid concussions, announced in unison, "We've seen enough action, captain. We're ready to go home — right here and now!"

April 20 — Around 2 a.m., the wind suddenly stiffened, and the sea was whipped into choppy, spray-blown whitecaps. The rolling of the Bullhead reminded us of the day nearly a month ago that we started this patrol.

We chalked up two dives with a total of more than 14 hours, rising to periscope depth at regular intervals to check on any possible Jap shipping. The seas were so turbulent that the boat broached several times by getting out of control momentarily when she was brought close to the surface.

It's amazing how much punishment the human body can take, yet continue to function with some degree of normalcy. The fliers were improving rapidly by now, and it was noticeable in the way they ate and joked. Lieuts. Charno and Sturm still possessed beautiful black eyes, but the swelling in their faces had receded, and they were full of energy. Following a shave and a sponge bath by a bearded "nurse," they tore into their food like starved men.

"This food is wonderful," they kept repeating amid the smacking of their lips. They had hot tomato soup, baked ham decorated with slices of golden pineapple, fresh bread, cherry meringue pie, and a sweet beverage made from coca cola syrup and ice water.

"Look, fellows," cried Charno. "Real ice! Man, we haven't had such chow since leaving home. How do you transfer from the Army to the Navy? I'd like to join immediately, but not for submarine duty. When we return to our base and spread the word around, there'll be Fifth Air Force pilots ditching by the dozen, just to be picked up and fed by submarines."

April 21 — There was no sleep for anyone, so tempestuous was the sea. On one occasion, I slid from my bunk onto the deck during a particularly heavy roll. I kept thinking of the time the men in the Boston Globe office told me I was a "lucky guy" to get such choice assignments. I must have cursed the paper a thousand times — once for every roll of the boat, but I wouldn't have missed this trip for anything.

Although Comdr. Griffith was running the Bullhead on the surface, he kept the boat rigged for diving. All hatches were closed to keep out water. The lookouts, oddly enough, stood periscope watches. The skipper wanted to submerge, but didn't dare to risk a dive in such heavy seas, for fear of capsizing.

We were shocked by the news of Ernie Pyle's death on Ie Shima, near Okinawa. I had had breakfast with him on Guam the morning after my return from a B-29 hop over Tokyo, and we had discussed my contemplated journey on a submarine.

"I've always been scared stiff of bombing missions," Ernie said, fingering the gray tufts of hair that fringed his head. "And I'd never go out in a submarine. I'd be scared even to walk through the inside of a sub tied up at a pier. I, personally, feel safer on dry land."

And yet, it was on dry land, tragically enough, that he was killed. His killer must have been an excellent marksman because the diminutive Pyle was such a small target.

April 22 — At religious services this afternoon in the forward torpedo room, a memorial prayer was dedicated to the three members of the B-25 crew who lost their lives earlier this week. Three faiths were represented among the victims: Catholic (White), Protestant (Pasledni) and Jewish (Cohen). All services are non-denominational and aimed at filling the desire for spiritual food and "nearness to God." They are not intended to in any way convert a man to a different belief.

April 24 — By now, Doc Scott was able to remove the stitches from the scalp of Sgt. Tukel. Lieut. Charno got up from his sack for the first time to walk around a bit unsteadily. He unfolded into a lanky, six foot one incher, and devoured spaghetti and meat sauce, and ice cream with the appetite of a growing boy. Come to think of it he is one, in a sense, for he's only 22.

To date, we have made more than 55 dives on this patrol. We have sighted and exploded four mines with 20- and 40-millimeter gunfire, and the skipper has to his personal credit a floating oil drum sunk with a carbine. (At first we had thought it to be a mine.) I sometimes wonder how many mines we have passed at night, and how close they were. I also wonder how many ships will be sunk by runaway mines after the war.

During the night, we dove twice on plane contacts, then submerged a third time off Pratas Reef to observe the tiny isle for the entire day. We saw three radio towers and a couple of weatherbeaten buildings, but failed to observe any smoke or other signs of life. At sunset, the skipper surfaced and gun crews lobbed a few more five inchers at the island.

"There's no sense in wasting any more ammunition," said Griff, as we pulled away. "I don't think there's anyone on the island, especially after the Fifth Air Force boys said they rendezvoused over the place."

* * * * *

The boat's engineer officer, genial Pat Doherty, has been in submarines 10 years, seven of them on the giant Narwhal before the war.

The Gloomy Dane, "Eric" Erickson, of Duluth, was principal of a small high school in Minnesota for two and a half years before joining the Navy. Until he arrived at New London, he had never seen an ocean or a submarine. He completed six successful patrols on the Tinosa and was depth charged on each one.

As welfare officer, Erickson acquired a small nickel slot machine whose profits were used to provide coke syrup, beer, cigars, and cigarettes for the crew. In addition, he holds the purse strings to an unofficial "slush fund," available for small personal loans to the men.

In addition to the captain, there are two other Annapolis graduates on the roster; Earl Hackman, from the class of 1943, and Ray Strassle, from the class of 1944, both of whom put in time on destroyers before joining the submarine service.

Junior officer aboard is Ens. Jack Simms II, 22, who lives on a small farm near Dallas. He attended Rice Institute and heard about subs in R.O.T.C. This is Tex's first war patrol and he has already made a name for himself as the Bullhead's champion chow hound and one of her best sack artists.

* * * * *

When the boat left New London, several members

of the crew formed the Beachcombers Club and agreed not to shave again until they returned to the States or were transferred to another boat. Upon joining the organization, a man deposited $5 with the treasurer and promised to pay each member $5 upon breaking the no-shaving rule.

At Key West, Marine sentries patrolling the entrance gates to the submarine base refused to pass the Bullhead's beavers through the gate without property passes, which had to be issued by an officer in this form: "one beard, black, property of seaman 1st class, Joe Doakes."

Clint Floyd, chief electrician's mate, of National City, Okla., the first president of the Beachcombers, was also the first man to shave his beard. He had to pay a mere $25 for the privilege since only six men comprised the total membership at the time.

Officers of the razor blade saving club are: Joseph W. Jones, electrician's mate 1st class, of Rule, Tex., president; John A. Roberts, electrician's mate 2nd class, of Niagara Falls, N. Y., vice president and treasurer, and John G. Cuccurullo, electrician's mate 2nd class, of Woonsocket, R. I., secretary.

Roberts said he scrupulously safeguarded the club's funds, but continually threatened to resign because the 15 members watched him so closely. As soon as they reach rest camp after this patrol, they plan to expend their capital on a bang-up party.

* * * * *

Many submariners report having strange dreams aboard the boat, as well as ashore. Some dream of their submarine heading toward the beach, then rolling along sand and knocking over trees and buildings. Other men dream of dodging torpedoes. The skipper is an inveterate "torpedo dodger," who works himself into complete exhaustion during his feverish nocturnal maneuvers. Even when he goes ashore, he ducks these weapons in his sub-conscious for weeks afterward.

13

April 25 — We are still grinding out mile after mile. A fifth mine was sighted, but the gun crews couldn't sink it even after scoring several hits. The skipper dove again in the middle of the night for a plane contact. Day in and day out, we continue to have our ups and downs.

April 26 — We have been anxiously awaiting orders from ComSubPac for the past few days, concerning our destination at the end of this war patrol. Scuttlebutt from all compartments threatens us with refits all over the Pacific, from the Aleutians to Australia, with a patrol of varying duration. This is our 30th day on station, excluding the time consumed in reaching the patrol area, and our relief submarine is due to arrive at sundown.

There are really only two places where the Bullhead can be ordered: Subic Bay, where Rear Admiral James Fife, Jr., Commander, Submarines, Southwest Pacific, recently established his headquarters, or Fremantle, Australia. The reason: SS-332 has been assigned to the Seventh Fleet. I don't have to take a poll to determine that everyone is keeping his fingers crossed in hope that Australia will be our destination.

Today, while patrolling miles from the China Coast, we sighted a fleet of Chinese fishing junks, seemingly topheavy and cumbersome, yet picturesque boats, bobbing up and down in the water like lobster pot buoys off the New England coast.

Comdr. Griffith was looking them over when Don Henriksen handed him an urgent dispatch he had just decoded. It was the news from headquarters. The

Bullhead was to leave her patrol area at sunset and proceed to Subic Bay. Her relief boat was already in the area.

Griff initialled the message. Suddenly he snapped his thin fingers and emitted a long low whistle. He called for Ray Strassle, and told him to check on the amount of food remaining in the boat's storage lockers and refrigerators.

"We're heading back to Subic tonight, Ray," explained the captain. "Figure out the amount of food we'll need to reach port, then have the surplus brought topside. We're going to conduct a lend-lease operation of our own."

An hour later, crewmen began to haul loaded cartons, tins, and assorted packages up the conning tower ladder to the deck, and forward to the bow. It was heavy work for the men and great beads of perspiration rolled down their pale faces.

They bore fresh meat, bread, pipe tobacco, rice, beans, packages of Nestle's hot chocolate mix, and a dozen other articles. I wondered what the Chinese would do with the chocolate powder. They could not read the directions; and I am certain they had never used the product before.

A medium size junk with several men shuffling around on deck was to receive our immediate attention. As we neared the homemade craft, the ageless Chinese stood unafraid against the deck railing and waved small fish at us to emphasize the fact that they were fishermen. They chattered unintelligibly among themselves. No doubt they had recognized us as Americans investigating the junks to determine whether they were fishermen or Japanese manned snoopers.

Although the craft appeared to be harmless, Griff did not take any chances. He had two machine guns manned, and ordered a couple of tommy guns and his .45 automatic brought to the bridge. The Bullhead rubbed alongside the boat; we were greeted with the pungent aroma of drying fish, Chinese style.

I experienced an indescribable thrill watching the faces of the Chinese when they spotted the big tins of rice and meat. They broke out in the broadest grins possible, exposed brownish teeth, wrinkled their faces, and again began to jabber amongst themselves, this time more excitedly than before.

They didn't speak English; we couldn't understand Chinese, so the ensuing lend-lease exchange had to be carried out entirely with wild gestures and frantic hand signals. They threw us a ragged line and hoisted just enough sail to close us. Our men heaved the chow at the Chinese; they reciprocated by offering the sub's yeoman and religious leader, Jim Brantley, a basket of dried fish that he refused to take.

When Brantley told the captain later about the offer, he snapped, "Dammit, you should have accepted a fistful of fish. That dried stuff is wonderful, and 'Scoop' would have liked the taste of it, purely as an experience."

Two roly poly brown babies were playing on the deck of the junk. Then a bronzed woman appeared with another baby clinging to her back in Indian papoose style. She was dressed in a long black kimono, and it was difficult to determine her age because the hair of many Chinese women remains glossy black for an unusually long time and their faces wrinkle slowly.

I judged the woman to be about 50. With the infant still hanging on for dear life, she wielded a boat hook and shouted commands as if she were the captain of the boat. The barefoot men moved quickly when she spoke. We didn't have any doubts, thereafter, as to the identity of the master. We cast off their lines, drifted apart a few feet, and waved good-by with our Diesels throbbing once more.

There was a short flurry of excitement when a lookout sighted an object in the water and reported it as a possible periscope. We could not detect a wake, and closer investigation proved the object to be an upright stick with a tiny, faded flag or colored cloth attached. Griff identified it as a fishing marker.

It's amazing how far these fragile looking junks dare to venture from land. If a storm had arisen suddenly, as they usually do in the China Sea, they could not have sought cover anywhere. The junks would have been forced to ride out the blow, and perhaps weather it the same way China has withstood 15 years of war — declared and undeclared.

Junks are perhaps the most picturesque type of boats in existence. They are easily identified by a high poop deck at the stern, and handmade, multi-section sails woven painstakingly from fiber and rigged on slender bamboo booms and arms. The Chinese operate the big rudder with a long tiller handle. Particularly characteristic of these junks are destructive toredo worm borings covering the exterior planking.

Griff focussed his attention next off our starboard quarter on a good sized junk that could have been another "Flying Dutchman," in view of the fact that nobody was on deck. There was not a soul in sight when the Bullhead nuzzled the sailing vessel. Finally, I spotted a grinning Chinese peering at us from behind the railing.

Evidently the rest of the crew had thought the Bullhead to be a Japanese submarine coming alongside to exact several baskets of fish as tribute, for in a moment three men climbed through the open hatches, hurriedly started to fill baskets with small fish, and hoisted them overhead. Several other fishermen then appeared. They scooped up more fish and attempted to pass us the baskets over the side.

Meanwhile, we were attempting to get the junk's crew to heave us a line. A brisk afternoon breeze had come up, and before they could realize that we were giving things to them instead of taking them, we began to drift apart. The Chinese were painfully slow in comprehending our mission. Finally, we had to throw them a line and pull their boat toward the sub.

When their eyes fell on our food, tobacco, and cans, they suddenly saw the light, and their facial expressions changed from fear and uneasiness to joy and understanding. And did they streak across their cluttered deck with flying speed to accept our supplies!

Fish were drying in the sun all over the deck. We could smell this junk 300 yards away; there was no mistaking her for anything but a fishing craft. A small overturned boat, covered with drying nets, lay amidships. Smoke drifted skyward lazily from a smouldering fire in a crude, open-air galley located aft on the starboard side. A pile of gnarled firewood was stacked neatly against the poop deck. It was nearly time for supper. I saw a pot of boiling rice containing chunks of fish.

As soon as the Chinese lifted the covers from the closed containers and saw the rest of the food, their faces lit up even brighter; they gave us "V" for Victory signs with the fingers of both hands. A lump arose in my throat and I felt tremendously proud to be an American.

It was probably the first time anyone had ever given these impoverished fishermen anything. Griff sighed and wished he had more food to spare, so he might distribute it to the other junks.

"These poor devils don't know there is such a high standard of living as ours," the skipper reflected gravely. "They have never seen a telephone or an electric refrigerator. Many of them have never seen any cash; they usually trade their fish for rice and other simple necessities of life. Perhaps, with all our time and labor saving gadgets and luxury, we are not as happy as they are aboard their dirty little junks — the only home they possess in the world."

You can always depend on American fighting men to be sympathetic, generous, and kind. If they are not the most liberal fellows in uniform, then they are mighty near the top. I have never seen a Yank who would not share his last can of C-rations with a buddy.

On Angaur in the Palau Islands, an 81st Division infantryman shared his canteen of warm water with me even though he did not know when he could get it refilled. And on Leyte, I watched scores of 96th Division troops hand over their rations and water to terrified Filipinos, who had fled from the jungle to the beach after our forces had established beachheads.

That is the American way.

*　*　*　*　*

The junk cast off our lines, and everyone aboard waved energetically at us. Our mission to mankind having been completed, Comdr. Griffith ordered full speed ahead and nosed the Bullhead toward Subic Bay. It was a wonderful feeling.

14

April 27 — It's remarkable how quickly the cheer-fulness radiated by the great news of our returning to port has permeated the Bullhead and her crew. Some-how the white lights seemed shades brighter, everyone's smile seemed inches broader, and there was a crispness of step that I hadn't seen before, except when the diving alarm sounded.

And no wonder! After the disappointment of a cancelled dash toward the Philippines, and after a series of rumored changes in the windup of our patrol, we were really on our way back at a fast clip. It was true at long last.

Although the crew were disappointed because they were not going to Australia for a merry rest period, I was content to put in at Subic. I would be able to reach Guam within 24 hours — if everything went well — and tear into a pile of mail that had accumulated (I hoped) during the past six weeks.

God must have known we had completed our war patrol, for He presented us with a well-nigh perfect day. The sea was as unruffled as the crew under fire. The cloudless sky was the same shade of tender blue as a newborn baby boy's blanket; a fat, friendly sun beat down upon everything within reach of its rays.

Everyone was awake and out of his sack earlier than usual. The plan of the day permitted unrestricted use of the showers; who cared if we ran out of fresh water, now that we could refill our tanks from a well stocked tender in 30 hours.

Throughout the sub, full beards and scraggly growths disappeared, as if by magic, under the sharp edges of razor blades. Even the Beachcombers forgot their pledges not to shave. Men slipped into clean dungarees; officers put on crisp khakis and wore visor caps for the first time.

Yeoman Brantley was busy typing the last pages of the captain's patrol report. Everyone was preparing to evacuate the boat as soon as she tied up. I stuffed my seabag last night with soiled clothing and unfolded my last clean change of khakis, which had to last until I reached Guam. One other man had all his gear ready; he was the only member of the crew to request transfer to surface craft.

Two fliers, Charno and Tukel, had improved sufficiently to make an inspection tour of the sub. Sturm's ankle was still badly swollen and thought to be fractured; open wounds remained on his left hand. Several of us contributed enough clean shorts, shirts, trousers, handkerchiefs, socks, and shoes to outfit the trio.

April 28 — Miles from the entrance to Subic Bay, a freshly painted DE picked us up to serve as our escort. Planes were reported from all quarters, but no one jumped toward the conning tower hatch, and no one became excited, because they were friendly planes and there was no doubt about it. Lookouts would report a B-24, then a C-47, another B-24, and an A-20, but nobody stirred. The new feeling of security was marvelous. It was like a new world. A world of peace.

At last, through the early morning haze that hovered over the mountain tops like smoke over a forest fire, we could observe the saw toothed profile of Luzon. The skipper climbed topside all decked out in his scrambled egg cap and last suit of starched khakis. He carried a roll of charts and attempted to pick out landmarks on the island, which he had not visited since late in 1941.

For the first time since going on patrol 10,000 miles ago, Griff gave orders to rig for surface and open all hatches. Cooks and bakers, who hadn't been on deck during the entire trip, pulled themselves up the ladder and blinked at everyone and everything.

Charno and Tukel, looking dapper in their newly acquired clothes, were helped up a forward hatch and seated in folding chairs, so they might bask in the sunshine and enjoy the fresh air. There wasn't the slightest roll as the Bullhead pushed along at a neat 18 knots through water as smooth as that schoolgirl complexion.

Soon we saw a long, irregular line of seaweed marking the tide boundary. We ran into a school of tiny, silvery flying fish that flashed friskily in and out of the water to provide unexpected entertainment.

Upon arriving at the entrance to Subic, speedy PT boats, operated by crews stripped to the waist, boiled across our bow and around our stern to get a good look at us. They waved enthusiastically; we exchanged greetings.

A few hundred yards ahead stretched the anti-submarine net built to keep out the likes of us. The squat net tender blinked a challenge for the recognition signal before granting permission to pass through. But they couldn't keep us out. We knew all the answers. Cruisers, destroyers, merchantmen, and various small craft anchored all over the big bay began to flash messages our way; I never did learn what all the "talking" was about.

A large launch then signalled us to slow down to enable a boarding party to come alongside. Five naval officers jumped aboard, made their way to the bridge, where they greeted the captain and offered directions for reaching our tender off Olangapo. Pale skinned crewmen continued to pour topside, until more than half our personnel were on deck.

Griff slowed the boat down to one third. We passed a gray tender with several subs tied up to her, continued to a second, the Howard W. Gilmore (named after the first submarine commander to receive the

Congressional Medal of Honor), then swung around slowly at 11 a.m., and nuzzled to the Sealion, the only submarine credited with sinking a Japanese battleship. Aboard the tender the ship's band struck up "Anchor's Aweigh," in brisk rhythm, and whipped into the "Army Air Force," in honor of the rescued fliers.

Waiting to board us from our sister ship, were Rear Admiral Fife; Commodore Edward S. Hutchinson, our division commander; two flight surgeons from the Fifth Air Force, and staff officers. While our lines were being made fast, they greeted Comdr. Griffith and the rest of the officers, then moved forward where the entire crew had been mustered and were standing at attention.

Admiral Fife pulled some papers from his pocket. He called for Joseph Wayne Jones, Thomas Philip Helferich, and William Edward Short to step forward, and awarded them Army Unit Citations for service in submarines in Manila at the outbreak of the war. It was the first formality they had experienced in weeks.

Two five gallon cans of chocolate ice cream and two cases of apples (unfortunately, the apples turned out to be wormy) were sent on board. But the major catastrophe, and a mighty blow it was to everyone's morale, centered about the ship's mail. Or rather the absence of it.

All the crew's personal mail and the boat's official mail had been missent somehow to Australia. No one could supply a reason for this disheartening error. It was SNAFU at its worst, and it put a damper on the day's pent up enthusiasm. The missing mail had a highly emotional effect on some men; they walked around with lumps in their throats and nearly broke out in tears.

When the Admiral and his party left the boat, the relief crew came aboard. They immediately began to unload the torpedoes, the first Griff had ever brought back from a patrol. Then came the ammunition and remaining supplies. All the soiled clothing, bed and table linen were sent to the Gilmore's laundry.

The Bullhead's personnel, meanwhile, filed aboard the tender for thorough physical examinations. They were given their initial doses of vile tasting atabrine to repress malaria, and were informed that, although they could visit their rest camp ashore during the day, they must return to the sub for the first three nights until the atabrine took effect.

The fliers went aboard the Gilmore for lunch before going ashore*.

I moved to the other tender to get a place to spend the night. With all the regular cabins filled with ship's officers and submariners, the First Lieutenant assigned me the captain's emergency cabin, a luxurious room with a comfortable mattress, coil springs and an air conditioning unit. Who could ask for more?

After chow, all hands boarded small boats for the trip to the rest camp. This proved to be another major disappointment. The rest camp was exactly what the name implied — a rest camp. The place had been under construction only a few weeks; there were several quonset barracks, a mess hall, a rough baseball diamond, a volleyball court, and a circus tent in which enlisted men could guzzle cold beer, and sweat it out nearly as quickly as they drank it. At night, the tent served as the camp theater. But there was little else. Men could swim in the tepid, fungi-filled bay but it appeared neither inviting nor clean. In fact, later, I found a sign forbidding swimming because the water was polluted.

---

*Tukel was bedded down in a tent on the beach. When a doctor showed up the next day, he informed the gunner that his X-ray was inoperative. He and Sturm were evacuated to a hospital on Leyte. Three days later, after numerous X-rays, medics diagnosed Tukel as having a broken back (compression fracture of the 9th and 10th dorsal vertebrae). His sternum was also cracked in two. As believed, Sturm's ankle was broken.

Comdr. Griffith and I visited the quonset hut occupied by submarine skippers. There he was delighted to find one of his classmates. The rest of the Bullhead's officers were also quartered in quonsets with beds and showers.

For the officers there was a Club Cisco — a collection of superb, eye filling nude photographs, a few unsteady tables and chairs, and a large, white electric refrigerator — all under one roof. Chit books sold for three dollars; beer cost a dime a can, with liquor available only after five o'clock.

Griff and I had a couple of brews, then boredom moved us to accompany his classmate for a walk in the hot sun. We strode uphill to visit a native style chapel under construction by Filipinos directed by Seabees. We sweat profusely and trudged through dust and mud, and when we returned to the tender at five o'clock, we felt the effects of no exercise and no sunshine during the patrol. We were completely exhausted, our leg muscles were stiff, and our faces were burned red.

Two hours later, Commodore Hutchinson, Griff, and I ferried over to Admiral Fife's flagship for dinner. The piece de resistance was a thick, juicy, flavorful filet mignon, one of the finest chunks of meat I had ever sunk my teeth into — anywhere. Fresh green broccoli, lemon pie (my favorite), and coffee completed the menu. Then we settled back in comfortable chairs to smoke Manila-rolled cigars and watch a private screening in the Admiral's cabin of "Fighting Lady," "A Night of Adventure," and some personal Kodachrome movies showing the destruction in Manila.

Admiral Fife announced that he had arranged my air transportation back to Guam the next day and my spirits zoomed 1,000 per cent. We sipped cold pineapple juice, chatted a while, and made our farewells.

The comforts of a private cabin and a soft bed were too much for me; I couldn't fall asleep. Besides, I had set the air conditioning on "cold" and nearly froze during the night with only a sheet for a cover.

As I was leaving the Gilmore in the morning, to go to San Marcellino airfield for a NATS (Naval Air Transport Service) flight to Guam via Mindoro and Samar Islands, Griff met me at the gangway and pulled me aside.

"Guess you were lucky, Scoop," he grinned. "Admiral Fife had sent a dispatch to Washington a few days ago, inquiring whether it was alright for other war correspondents to go out on patrol. The reply from CominCh (Fleet Admiral Ernest J. King) arrived last night. It read:

WAR CORRESPONDENTS MAY NOT REPEAT MAY NOT GO ON SUBMARINE WAR PATROLS.
                                                                    KING

SECOND WAR PATROL

1

FOUR days after the Bullhead put in to Subic Bay, the crew's mail arrived from Australia by special plane, thereby saving the day. These letters from home — and these letters alone — prevented the men's 15 day stay on the beach from becoming an utter catastrophe. Some read all their mail at one sitting; others rationed themselves to one letter a day, so they might stretch the thrill of a new letter daily well into their next patrol.

Earl Hackman, Ray Strassle and Don Henriksen spent a few days winding up their studies, then took the examinations for designation as "Qualified in Submarines." All passed with flying colors.

Incidentally, investigation of the April 8 bombing of the Bullhead proved the culprit was a Liberator. Submarine officers lodged vigorous protests with the Army Air Force.

Subic Bay proved to be a pretty dreary place for recreation, but the men were promised a refit in Fremantle after their next patrol. (Admiral Fife believed in having submarines alternate their refits between Subic and Fremantle.) The highlights of their hours of leisure ashore were a gala beer party and a free hitting baseball game between the engineers and the deck force. Keith Phillips managed to round up two idle LCI's, and broke the monotony further with an overnight sight-seeing tour to Manila for all hands.

SECOND WAR PATROL

Comdr. Griffith located the home where he and his wife had lived for two years. His identification of the ruins was remarkable, in view of the fact that only a dining room wall remained standing. There was little else to see in the ravished city besides widespread destruction, but even that was a change of scenery for the restless men.

The Bullhead fared much better than her crew. She had her face lifted, and with the new paint job, she looked just as good as new. Below deck, she was completely overhauled. Her tired engines had been overdue; they required new bearings, rings and cylinder heads. New torpedoes, ammunition, and fresh food were loaded.

May 13 — The refit was completed and the bored, weary crew were anxious to move back on their boat and get underway. A new ensign, Joseph J. Parpal, fresh out of Submarine School, reported aboard for his first patrol and took over the wardroom bunk I had vacated.

For the next eight days, the old man conducted a rigorous training program off the coast of Luzon, firing the guns, practicing speedy dives, and working with other warships to test sound and radar gear, and to sharpen up on approaches to targets.

May 21 — The Bullhead and her proud crew departed at 1 p.m. for their second war patrol to wage unrestricted submarine warfare against the Japs in the Gulf of Siam and the Java Sea.

May 23 — Paul Gossett ruined the tranquility of a sunny afternoon by reporting an object that looked like a rubber raft with a man in it about three miles dead ahead.

"I think I can see someone paddling," he said, peering through his binoculars.

The captain pulled himself out of his sack to go

topside in slippers and shorts. He had already ordered the rescue team on deck for what he expected would be another dashing rescue of aviators. Lines were made ready; men slipped into Mae Wests and rushed around to take their places. On approaching the boat, however, all that Gossett found was a floating palm tree.

"We got a laugh out of the incident," said the skipper, "but it proved the men were alert. I'd rather have someone report a bird as a possible plane, than get trapped on the surface by a plane he might have identified as a bird but didn't."

At 3:10, a lookout sighted a distant vessel that was identified as a non-United States submarine. Griff looked her over carefully until she submerged; then he dove and poked around at periscope depth. An hour and a half later, the target surfaced 3,000 yards away and crossed the Bullhead's bow at 1,200 yards, apparently unaware that another sub was within a mile of her. The old man positively identified her as British and wrote laconically in his report, "We were in position for a good shot."

May 24 — Gunnery, fire control, and diving drills continued until this noon, when the sub was 54 miles off Pulo Condore en route to the Gulf of Siam.

The skipper, who had been nervously awaiting word of the birth of his first child, finally received the announcement by radio, and joyously passed out cigars. Unbeknownst to him, the crew had prepared a huge three layer cake completely covered with glistening white frosting and inscribed:

"Virginia Lee Griffith — Launched May 22, 1945."

The patrol plan called for the Bullhead to cover the south central part of the Gulf with the Bergall (SS-320) and the Kraken (SS-370), which had been in the area three weeks. Two other boats, one of them the Icefish (SS-367), were assigned to the northern area. As an accommodation, Griff had taken aboard five sacks of mail for the Bergall just before leaving Subic. At 10 p.m., he established radio contact with her and arranged to rendezvous the next day.

May 25 — SS-332 entered her patrol area, sighted and closed the Bergall shortly before noon, but Comdr. John M. Hyde, her skipper and wolf pack co-ordinator, was anxious to wait until dark for the mail transfer. Despite the fact that the Japs' claws have been trimmed short, he was not willing to stick his neck out needlessly.

The two subs finally rendezvoused at eight o'clock, with the Bergall coming alongside to pick up the sacks and deliver wolf pack instructions to Comdr. Griffith. The meeting was brief and the boats parted almost immediately. Twenty minutes later, the radio silence was broken by a stream of salty curses from the Bergall. It seemed that 90 per cent of the letters in the five sacks had been incorrectly sorted and were for the Boarfish, patrolling in the Java Sea.

A year ago, American submarines were reluctant to rendezvous with one another in enemy territory. They rarely operated boldly on surface. Transferring mail at sea was virtually unheard of, and breaking the strict radio silence would have brought down the wrath of the pack commander on the careless skipper. But everything was different now. Our valiant skippers thumb their noses at the Japs and dare them to come out and fight.

May 26 — Business was quiet all day, except for a small Jap float plane that was detected five miles to the north at sundown and forced the Bullhead to dive. That's when the Japs conduct most of their reconnaissance patrols; they also prefer the early morning hours.

After dark, the Bergall again slipped alongside to return the mail belonging to the Boarfish and beg for the loan of a spare motion picture projection lamp to replace their burned-out one. The cigar-shaped terrors of the sea rolled easily in the swells while Jim Collins, electrician's mate 3rd class, pored through his movie equipment and came up with the desired article.

Before hitting the sack, Griff bemoaned his present dilemma, the same one he and other submarine skippers have had to contend with since the early days of the war.

"If we patrol submerged on station," he reasoned, "we lose too much coverage. If we patrol on surface, we get spotted and may as well not be there. The Japs know we have subs in the Gulf of Siam. Their problem is to find out how many and where we patrol. Woe is me."

May 27 — Two more meetings with the Bergall. Yesterday, Philippines-based search planes sighted two Marus, small Jap freighters, steaming from Singapore Strait toward Great Redang Island. The pack plans to try to intercept them.

May 28 — The assumption that the Japs are well aware of the presence of American submarines in the Gulf was proved this morning when they jammed the pack frequency for several hours.

Griff took the Bullhead into shallow water and reconnoitered inshore, about 1,000 yards from the southern limits of the Great Redang Anchorage, formerly one of the Japs' busiest transshipment points. He didn't see a ship, not even a junk. A B-24 snooper, circling overhead, reported he couldn't find a trace of the Marus, either. For all he knew, the Japs might have run their craft ashore and hidden them in the palms.

* * * * *

A month ago, when Griff checked the commissary report covering the Bullhead's first patrol, he found that the boat had gone in debt due to the high cost of food in the States and some injudicious purchasing of too much expensive meat. The food used had cost nearly $1,000 more than the sub's allowance; that was an unhealthy situation, to say the least.

It was therefore necessary to start economizing and being more careful of their food. The skipper asked Keith Phillips to talk to the crew about it.

"Tell them the refrigerator will continue to remain open all the time," said Griff, "but advise them to try not to waste food as I am held personally responsible for the commissary deficit."

Tonight the exec reported the crew had collected $200 among themselves and wanted to help pay off the debt.

"I certainly appreciate their good intentions, Keith," the captain said, "but we can't pay a deficit that way. Tell the boys to save the money for a party in Perth."

This incident is typical of the high morale of the crew.

2

May 29 — Comdr. Griffith has been suffering from dysentery since leaving Subic. The great strain of conducting this patrol in shallow water close to shore does not help his condition and he has dropped 10 pounds. Several other cases have been reported among the crew.

Amid scores of small junks and tiny native craft sailed by dark skinned Malayans, the Bullhead rendezvoused with the Bergall and the Kraken. These small native boats are unique affairs, resembling a cross between a Chinese junk and a Philippine catamaran. A few appeared to be nothing more than hollowed-out logs with outriggers.

The three skippers bemoaned the absence of Japanese shipping in their area. Then Comdr. Hyde ordered a different disposition of the pack and the underwater raiders went on their way.

Later, an Army search plane reported two tugs towing five barges about 50 miles north of the Bullhead and heading in her general direction.

Memorial Day, May 30 — Griff submerged in 15 fathoms of water at dawn off Hilly Cape-Patani Yering. He crossed his fingers and hopefully awaited the arrival of the small enemy craft. Nothing came his way by noon so he surfaced to hear the bad news. The Bergall had seen the tug and barges first, taken pot shots and sunk them. There wasn't a thing left for the Bullhead.

By mid afternoon another report had crackled in. This time a large sailing vessel was hugging the beach 10 miles from the Bullhead. Griff dove to periscope depth and watchfully felt his way up the coast in search of his target for tonight's Memorial Day celebration.

The old man picked nervously at his dinner. A half hour later he climbed up the conning tower ladder and pushed his eyes against the rubber eyepiece of a periscope. He swung it around slowly and suddenly stopped.

"I see her now," he announced. "Holy mackerel! What a strange rig!"

The craft was a two masted lugger that resembled a big sailing barge more than anything else because of her beam.

Griff surfaced at 7:10 at battle stations — gun action, and ordered full speed ahead so he might get between the lugger and the beach, and prevent her from deliberately running aground.

In 15 minutes he opened fire from 2,200 yards with the five incher, 20- and 40-millimeters. The first big shell put the lugger down by the bow. After an even dozen rounds of five inchers, 16 rounds of 40-millimeter and 240 of 20-millimeter fire, the sailing vessel was completely ablaze. Finally, with a grand display of holiday fireworks, she went to the bottom at 7:30.

Griffith estimated the lugger at 150 tons. She carried studsails and a large jib, was approximately 150 feet long, with an unusually wide beam of 40 feet. The target wasn't much as targets go, but the Japs are scraping the bottom of the barrel, and submarine skippers do not have much choice in the matter.

The Bullhead cleared the shore in only six fathoms, practically running aground during the attack, and dove in deeper water to flush out her number four fuel ballast tank. The score: Bullhead — 150 tons.

May 31 — Griff got permission to search Singora Anchorage, where enemy shipping usually anchored for a breathing spell at night. He asked Comdr. Tom Henry of the Kraken to take his place in the scouting line, then sped all full ahead for Patani Roads. Entering the Roads at nine o'clock, he followed the six and seven fathom curves to Singora. There he carefully skirted the big minefield, swept the coast for miles, and found absolutely nothing.

"I wish we were amphibious," the skipper grumbled in the wardroom, "then we might have an opportunity to damage Jap installations ashore."

June 1 — A single engine float plane was sighted heading north up the Malayan coast about 15 miles away. It was swinging in a wide circle so Griff ducked beneath the surface. When he popped up an hour later, the seaplane was still in sight.

"I think he's covering something," said Griff. "Let's get the extra 20-millimeter and .50 calibre guns mounted topside."

An hour and a half before sunset he set course for Patani Roads. At 5:55, the Bullhead dove for a Pete picked up five miles away. When the sub resurfaced in 20 minutes, a lookout sighted wreckage from the lugger they had sunk the day before yesterday. Her stern hung at a crazy angle with the mainmast and shrouds showing. Apparently her bow was resting on the bottom because the fathometer registered only 126 feet of water. Griff decided to give the gun crews more target practice and ordered the 20- and 40-millimeter guns manned. They soon leveled the debris to the waterline.

June 4 — In accordance with prearranged plans, the Bullhead moved to a new patrol station south of Anambas Island, between Pulo Rittan and Doemdoem, to establish an offensive scouting line in support of the landings by Australian troops at Brunei Bay, Borneo, scheduled a week hence. This was the beginning of an extremely dull week, uneventful except for the sighting of three American patrol planes.

Friday, June 8 — The following notice was posted in the Control Room and the Crew's Mess this morning:

SECOND WAR PATROL

ALL HANDS:

We started holding Church Services on Sunday because it was felt that most of us wanted it.

Last patrol we had a good attendance. The last two Sundays we have had about 10 (including officers and men). I have no desire to coerce you to attend Church; but I can assure you that the 15 minutes it takes to attend Church will repay you a hundred-fold in contentment and a feeling of well being.

Jesus said, "Where two or three are gathered together in my name; there will I be also."

We will continue our services as long as they are desired and you are all earnestly requested to attend.

Respectfully,

W. T. GRIFFITH
Commander, USN
Commanding

Enough said?

Sunday, June 10 — At two, the forward torpedo room was jammed by a more than 100 per cent increase in attendance in response to the "gentle" prodding by Comdr. Griffith who, incidentally, delivered the sermon on "Jesus and the Coming Judgment." Following the service, a "Sing-festal" of hymns and spirituals was held with Adrianus Schellinkhout serving as musical director.

June 13 — Everything was going along well until a radar operator picked up a contact at 10,000 yards at 2:15 a.m. From the size of the solid pip on the screen, it appeared to be a submarine. Griffith, still weak from dysentery, pulled himself out of his sack to investigate.

The contact was in the vicinity where a British submarine*, the Taciturn, would have been if she were still on station. But she was supposed to have left the area 15 hours before.

---

*British and Dutch submarines were working in force with the Americans in the Pacific in 1945. They destroyed many Jap warships and merchantmen, beginning on December 24, 1941, when a Dutch sub sent torpedoes into the destroyer Sagiri, off Sarawak.

OVERDUE AND PRESUMED LOST

If there's anything feared by a submarine skipper, it is meeting another submarine. The craft have such low silhouettes that they are difficult to detect. And when they have been picked up, they are a mighty elusive target to catch and hit. Of course, the disadvantages also hold true for the enemy.

The skipper tried to contact the Taciturn by radio but could not raise her. After two hectic hours he sent out word of contacting an unidentified submarine. But the vigilant Taciturn was not taking any risks. The British sub continued to play the nerve wracking game of hide and seek; indeed, she really lived up to her name as defined by Webster — habitually silent; not given to conversation.

Finally, Griff sent another dispatch to the Taciturn's commander. This time he gave the strange submarine's position, said he was going to attack, and asked if that were he. At 4:50 the Bullhead's radio receivers came to life for the first time in 155 uncomfortable minutes.

"Yes, me," came the meek reply from the unloquacious British submarine, and everyone breathed easier. The Taciturn didn't lose any time in taking off for her new assignment.

June 14 — The pilot of a PB4Y search plane circling overhead politely inquired whether he could do anything for the submarine. Griff asked him to look over the Anambas Islands for possible shipping, but a negative report was delivered.

June 15 — A plane identified as either a Sally or a Betty crossed the sub's stern about 10 miles distant, heading in a southwesterly direction.

Orders arrived for the Bullhead to move to the western end of the Java Sea. Accordingly, she left her post at seven o'clock, for Batavia via Karimata Strait.

June 17 — Submerged at dawn off the Java Coast just east of Batavia in 14 fathoms. Surfaced at sundown and headed for Pamanukare Anchorage, where Griff snooped only 8,000 yards from the docks without seeing anything except a small junk and a buoy. A submariner's search for enemy shipping was becoming increasingly futile.

June 18 — SS-332 arrived off St. Nicholas Point, West Java, near the spot where the American cruiser Houston and the Australian cruiser Perth were sunk by the Japs in 1942. Like the wise fisherman who continues to shift his boat from place to place until he finds a good fishing spot, Griff was moving around in search of Japs.

The captain's dysentery has taken a turn for the worse. For two days now he has been too weak to leave his cabin for the bridge. But he finally dragged himself with difficulty to the conning tower, after Keith Phillips rushed breathlessly into his cabin and announced, "We've just sighted the strangest looking mess I've ever seen. I hate to ask this, Captain, but I think you ought to come up for a look."

Griff fastened his eyes to the periscope, blinked a couple of times in amazement, and straightened up with obvious effort.

"Christ, Keith," he said, "is that the same thing you saw?"

The exec returned to the scope for a peek, then replied, "That's it, Captain. Looks like a floating island, doesn't it?"

The old man took another peek, and said, "I think I see what it is now. It's a camouflaged coastal vessel. See those palm trees on deck, and the green fronds decorating her masts, rigging and sides. They're well camouflaged against aircraft. Sure is the damnedest rig I've ever set eyes on. Let's prepare to surface, Keith. Battle stations — gun action!"

When the Bullhead's prow broke the surface at 9:17, the Jap craft immediately headed for the beach, but the sub's third five incher stopped her dead in her tracks. Thirty seven rounds of big stuff and over 300 rounds of small arms fire polished off the camouflaged job in 13 minutes.

"I'll never forget that first startling look at her through the periscope," said Comdr. Griffith. "When we surfaced, I identified her as a small, steel hulled Diesel Sugar Charlie. She was flying the Japanese flag and had perhaps 50 men on board."

This sinking added 700 tons to the Bullhead's score, making it 850 tons.

Fate had decreed June 18 to be an eventful day for the big American submarine. Two hours after polishing off the "floating island," her skipper sighted a big transport plane circling an airfield near St. Nicholas Point prior to going in for a landing. And 20 minutes later lookouts saw a small patrol craft poking around near the scene of the sinking.

"Then we sighted the mast and deck house of another patrol boat coming from Sunda Point and carefully hugging the shore," Griff went on. "Suddenly the Japs reversed course. They were so near the beach I couldn't figure out why they didn't run aground."

At sundown, the Bullhead surfaced to charge batteries. An uncomfortably bright moon really kept her lookouts and OD on the alert. They called Griff to the bridge at 9:20 after sighting two columns of heavy black smoke. Soon he made out two small vessels and two escorts. Strangely enough, they were proceeding on a straight course.

The Japs were always unpredictable. Here they were escorting two merchantmen on a moonlit night; yet they violated convoy rules by not controlling their smoke which could be sighted many miles away. One of the most rigid rules of war insists that all ships operate with a minimum of smoke. Another requires convoys to zigzag, but this group was steaming so close to land, it was impossible for them to do so.

Griff submerged at 10:10 to ponder the situation.

The moon was too bright for him to make a surface approach, he reasoned. And he couldn't very well use torpedoes, because the vessels were too small and did not ride deep enough in the water. Amid glances at the convoy through the periscope, the skipper planned to let the craft pass him at 1,000 yards, then fire torpedoes at them, if possible, or battle surface.

At 10:26 the convoy was 6,000 yards away. Griff was watching the situation closely when the ships suddenly changed course and turned toward the beach where they milled about in utter confusion.

"Guess they've picked us up and gotten scared," Griff grumbled.

They swung around again at 9,000 yards, then reversed course to return to their anchorage, thus dropping the asbestos curtain on what might have been an interesting show.

3

June 19 — Last night was peaceful for a change; the Bullhead managed to recharge her batteries without incident and submerged at dawn off St. Nicholas Point. But two meals were destined to be delayed today.

Breakfast was rudely interrupted when the OD reported a column of black smoke. At first, the stack from which the smoke was pouring seemed to be sitting on a 1,000 ton freighter. Closer up, though, the vessel looked like a 250 ton patrol craft, similar to our PC's. This one was zigzagging and appeared to be a conversion job of some tuglike vessel. Through the periscopes, lookouts could see a three inch gun forward, a radar dome atop a single mast, and two well filled depth charge racks. Some 4,000 yards ahead of the sub, the patrol boat began an intensive search, which she suddenly interrupted to scoot off in the direction of Batavia.

The Bullhead continued to patrol at periscope depth until two small Jap picket boats sped past her at 1,000 yards to throw a monkey wrench into the crew's lunch. Each craft carried a 37-millimeter gun forward and ashcan racks aft. Griff identified them as former Dutch torpedo boats captured by the Japs during the East Indies campaign.

A few moments later, lookouts sighted additional telltale trails of smoke on the horizon and soon the targets hove into sight. Both were steel hulled; the first, a large SC type coastal vessel of 700 tons, and the second, a 500 tonner. And following them were the two picket boats that had been sighted earlier.

Griff surfaced and commenced firing with the five incher and the 40-millimeter gun at 2:21 p.m. The

midget escorts immediately started to close the submarine. Then they suddenly changed course as if they
had seen Al Capp's Lena the Hyena. There was great
confusion and the boats headed toward Banten Anchorage.

The larger target, meanwhile, was sunk at exactly
2:30, sliding under with great clouds of hissing steam
enveloping her bow. The Bullhead's gun crews had
eaten up too much ammunition in the first attack, since
the big shells were hitting topside instead of the hull.
Now, with only nine rounds of five inch projectiles remaining, Griff went off on a final wild shooting spree
against the second Sugar Charlie that had already
rounded a point of land and was trying desperately to
run aground. With three hits splitting open her stern,
the SC shuddered to a stop on the beach and her after
part sank several feet.

A small coastal town was in sight. Griff spotted
two 300 ton craft tied up to a rickety dock, and a few
one story buildings. He moved in closer and ordered
the gunners to spray the dock area with 40-millimeter
fire and save the last six rounds of big stuff for the
boats. A burst of flame leaped from one when a five
inch shell struck her; two direct hits on the second
vessel set her ablaze also.

Having expended most of his ammunition and shot
up practically everything in sight, Griff swung the Bullhead around and headed for good water.

In less than an hour, lookouts sighted a fast moving
Pete on the starboard beam about 10 miles away. The
old man dove the boat to await darkness. Four distant
depth charges thundered through the water during the
afternoon, but they were too far off to disturb anyone.

* * * * *

The superb sense of humor of the American fighting
man has always managed to help him through the most
difficult and unpleasant situations. Being able to ap-

preciate a humorous situation is of paramount importance, especially on a submarine.

Comdr. Griffith described an amusing incident that occurred during one of his patrols on the Bowfin. The sub was laying less than two miles off an enemy held island at dusk. On the bridge stood two officers so entranced by the Melanesians' native huts, the palms, the jungle, and the local odors being wafted seaward that they were neglecting their watch. They didn't even notice the captain climb topside.

But they sure enough heard him yell, "Goddammit, if you don't pay more attention to your watch, I won't take you sightseeing any more!"

Another time, one of the skipper's commissioned watchstanders reported sighting a destroyer supposedly traveling at 15 knots. He rang up flank speed, called for battle stations, and notified the skipper. Griff took over on the bridge, picked up his binoculars, peered through them and saw — a tiny island!

* * * * *

June 22 — Early this morning the Bullhead picked up a small schooner with a junk rig 150 miles from land. Griff had all the guns manned before moving in close to investigate. The boat carried light cargo stacked amidships and probably displaced about 25 tons. Her crew of 10, all light skinned Malayans, were most vociferous in their protestations of innocence and friendship. The skipper did not believe it reasonable that a Jap would venture so far from land without an escort, and permitted the boat to pass.

June 24 — One of the most unusual incidents of this patrol took place in mid afternoon, when a lookout reported masts on the horizon, bearing, three zero eight, 15 miles.

The target was a large ship, from 8,000 to 10,000 tons. Although the huge red crosses on her hull professed innocence, she was following a zigzag course and otherwise maneuvering in a most radical manner. Griff continued to watch her closely throughout the afternoon. Finally, the Japanese ship began to blink her mast lights.

"The Hardhead had reported her to be a hospital ship," said the skipper, "but she was violating the instructions for mercy vessels by zigzagging, interfering with and embarrassing our operations. We could see red lights on her, though she should have carried white. I considered she should be sunk and asked for permission from headquarters to fire our torpedoes. After waiting three and a half hours for a reply, I abandoned the chase. Just as well, because when the reply came, it was 'No'."

This is another instance of the Japanese violating the code of international law and getting away with it. Had the Bullhead sunk the so-called hospital ship, the Nips would have screamed, "Unfair! Unfair!!" But anyone would have declared the vessel a legitimate military target because of her actions.

June 25 — The Bullhead and other submarines are now patrolling north of Lombok Strait (east of Java between Bali and Lombok Island). Griff submerged, but was forced to surface soon thereafter by a serious leak in the maneuvering room.

"The water is going over our circulating equipment," reported Pat Doherty. "Seems to be coming from our circulating water line."

The leak was caused by wartime construction, he pointed out. Instead of a steel test plug, the builders has used a cast iron one that had been eaten in two by rust. Doherty fashioned a steel replacement, better than the original, and the sub was able to dive again to await a target.

Griff didn't have to wait very long before a large two masted coastal schooner, flying a double jib, came into view. He surfaced with the schooner on the port bow and saw another small vessel barely moving in the shadow of the beach on the Bali side.

Looking over the boat from 15 yards, he noticed that the deck cargo included boxes and drums. She also had an auxiliary engine, which was a virtual guarantee that she was in the service of the Japs. The skipper drafted a dispatch to the Hardhead about the schooner and started out after the other boat, even though he had only small arms ammunition left.

At 8:05 p.m., SS-332 caught up with the fleeing craft and found her to be a medium Sugar Charlie, a coastal merchantman of an estimated 300 tons. The sub commenced firing with her 20- and 40-millimeters and .50 calibers. Griff gave the "Cease fire" order two minutes later, when the target was burning beautifully fore and aft. Oil and gasoline in her cargo exploded with spectacular bluish-white flashes and sent black clouds of smoke mushrooming skyward. While the sub was circling the damaged ship, lookouts heard the cries of men clinging to debris in the water.

"They sounded like natives so we picked them up," explained Griff. "They proved to be 10 Javanese; we locked them in an empty magazine and treated two for slight burns."

One native spoke Dutch. Subsequent inquiries among the submarine crew led to the amazing discovery that Schellinkhout had been born in the Netherlands and could converse with the survivor. During several talks with him, Schellinkhout obtained considerable intelligence information.

The natives were happy at their rescue from the sea, but they were especially joyous at their liberation from the Japs. They said four Japs were aboard their oiler; the captain, engineer, and two soldiers. Two of them had been wounded during the attack. The others probably went down with the boat.

Schellinkhout also learned that the Japs conducted

a training school on Java, where they shanghaied innocent natives and forced them to learn to operate small craft. The Javanese were listed on the books for high rates of pay, but they said they never saw the money.

When Comdr. Griffith contacted the Hardhead to tell of his success, the other sub told of nailing the two masted schooner near Ambat. And at 11 p.m., the oiler was still sinking slowly, and burning and exploding at intervals.

June 26 — The end of the sub's second patrol has been interrupted by a radar contact on two ships at 17,800 yards. With the sea becoming rough and the moonlight glaring from the water, Griff radioed the two other subs in his immediate area that he wouldn't attack until one of them also made contact.

Two hours later, the Blueback reported contacts on two targets that appeared to be small Jap mine layers. Griff zigzagged into position and fired a spread of six fish from the bow tubes. Two broached harmlessly in the deep troughs and threw up big sprays even more noticeable than the white caps. The remainder tore harmlessly past the targets. But the confused Japs saw their wakes and one turned toward the Bullhead at 1,100 yards. Griff dove immediately, rigged for depth charges, and started evasive tactics.

A few minutes later, four ashcans exploded with sharp concussions approximately 3,000 yards away. Everyone waited with bated breath for more depth charges, but they didn't materialize. When Griff rose to periscope depth just before midnight, one minelayer was still in sight.

June 27 — After losing contact with the target from 12:10 to 12:45 a.m., the Bullhead picked up another pip. Then the Blueback reported she was diving for an attack.

"I figured I had contact with the minelayer we had fired on earlier," said Griff. "The target stopped, circled us, and at 1:40 we heard a few more distant depth charge concussions. At 1:49, the mine layer was blown to bits from the Blueback's torpedoes, and disappeared."

But the action for this busy night was not yet over. Radar operators picked up another surface contact at 13,000 yards at 4:18. The old man ordered all ahead full and began to close the target rapidly. At 4:22, only 9,000 yards separated the Bullhead from the contact. The range was only 5,400 yards six minutes later.

The vessel was zigzagging. That maneuver and her low silhouette made positive identification most difficult. Griff ordered his gun crews to battle stations and continued to stalk the enemy.

By 6 a.m., the target had moved out to 12,000 yards. The skipper guessed her to be a small mine layer or a Chidori. He figured the Jap could see the sub and planned to shoot fast once he headed over.

Lookouts sighted a U. S. submarine 10 minutes later about 15,000 yards ahead of the Bullhead, then a second sub just ahead of the target. The sun rose at 6:24 and Griff was certain that the target had him clearly in sight.

"He has no intention of approaching me," wrote the skipper in his battle report. "I don't have enough speed to close him. This is a situation for the books. With the two other submarines ahead, I had better pull astern as I do not have enough fuel to keep up full power for a day."

The Bullhead dropped back and left the target to the mercy of the other subs. Griff changed course for Lombok Strait and passed astern of the mine layer at 9,000 yards.

"He could have taken a pot shot at us with his guns," said Griff, "but he didn't. We finally submerged in North Lombok Strait to rest up after a strenuous but disappointing night."

At dusk he surfaced and searched Ambat Anchorage

and the northeast coast of Bali. Not a ship could be seen from 800 yards. Not even a Balinese dancing girl.

During their short visit the 10 Javanese preferred plain meat and beans three times a day to the regular crew's mess. They were anxious not to fall into enemy hands again and told interpreter Schellinkhout where they desired to be turned loose. Griff obliged by putting them afloat in a rubber boat about six miles west of Ambat.

The Bullhead entered narrow Lombok Strait at 7:40 and completed an uneventful transit of the treacherous, shallow water two hours later. The sunset was gorgeous, with golden shafts extending into the pale blue sky. Japs, depth charge attacks, enemy shipping, and snooping planes were left far behind and everyone relaxed peacefully in his bunk to enjoy the first good night's sleep in days.

June 28 — Although the equator was crossed over a week ago, everyone was too busy to engage in the usual ritual. King Neptune, in the person of Pat Doherty, did not come aboard until this afternoon, when the submarine passed south of the Malay Barrier and entered the Indian Ocean en route to Fremantle.

Pat's white robe was fashioned from a mattress cover, his crown from cardboard, and his staff from a swab handle, with the tines made from copper tubing. He decreed that the Pollywogs who had crossed the imaginary line for the first time should undergo a 24 hour probationary period before their introduction to the royal domain.

June 29 — From one to four o'clock, King Neptune and his royal party received, examined, and indoctrinated nearly 50 Bullheaders into the royal domain with a proper ceremony. Well, as proper a ceremony as could be held below deck on a submarine.

Short was the royal baby (and a good one), Bill Smith was royal priest, Ed Engebretsen was navigator, while

Keith Phillips sat in the prosecutor's chair. The following served as cops or bears: George Bell, Ray Church, Tom Helferich, Joseph Jones and Bill Peart.

The initiation was hilarious and rough, as all initiations should be. All the victims were found guilty as charged. Prosecutor Phillips asked the initiates embarrassing questions thought up by the members of his court. Upon voicing an incorrect answer, they were worked over by the cops and bears. Then they were consoled by the priest who gave them a healthy shot of electricity when he blessed them.

One by one, the novices were placed flat on their backs on the operating table and given a shot of some vile tasting mixture for anesthesia. Most men held it in their mouth. The patients were "operated" on by the royal doctor wielding an electrified knife that tickled and forced them to swallow their medicine. Needless to say, somewhere along the line the royal barber gave the Pollywogs' scalps a complete going-over with suds and razor.

Prior to the ceremony most of them were required to dress in some silly uniform for lunch. Some enlisted men wore dress blue jumpers minus their trousers, while officers had to wear dress blues. Jack Simms had to deliver a 10 minute speech titled "What is Wrong With Texas," and was followed by Paul Gossett who spoke overly long and had to be carried bodily out of the wardroom to end his discourse.

July 2 — The Bullhead completed her second interesting war patrol at 10:50 a.m., when her lines were made fast to the submarine tender USS Clyte in Port Fremantle. Her score: 1,850 tons of enemy shipping destroyed, 1,300 tons damaged. She cruised 11,623 miles in 43 days.

OVERDUE AND
PRESUMED LOST

1

THE U. S. Navy Base at Fremantle opened its heart
for the Bullhead, just as it did for every returning
submarine. Immediately following the greetings, physical exams, and other preliminaries, the entire crew was
paid off and the base beer hall opened for a "welcome
home" party. Navy alphabet flags decorated the huge
hall; several colorful BULLHEAD and WELCOME
banners hung from the center rafters. Best of all,
everything was on the house. Everything meaning all
the iced beer a man could drink. And this was atomic
Australian brew, not the weak, green stateside stuff
served at mid-Pacific bases.

"Such a welcome always brings an exalted sensation,"
said Jim Brantley. "No matter how many times a man
experiences this, he always feels as though nothing more
thrilling has ever happened to him. It helps a fellow
to think that 'it was worth it'."

After the miserable refit at Subic Bay, the two weeks
of parties and recreation in Perth made the land down
under seem like paradise or Utopia. There were beer
parties, horseback riding parties, theater and hunting
parties. Enlisted men lived at the Hyde Park Hotel
taken over by the Navy and gathered daily in the pub
to quaff Aussie ale. Then there were off the record
parties, informal and unscheduled, continued in some-

one's room after the pub closed by procuring a supply of beer and lugging it upstairs in cases. Officers stayed at the nearby Adelphi Hotel.

Texas Jack Simms took his examination for qualification in submarines and passed with flying colors.

He made the mistake of riding a horse to celebrate and Comdr. Griffith had to present the dolphins and combat insignia to him in his room at the Hollywood Hospital (an absurd name for an Australian hospital). It seemed that the spirited animal, unable to understand Jack's Texas drawl, headed for a tree. Simms hurriedly yanked one foot out of the stirrup. The horse swerved sharply from the tree and the Texas cowboy parted company, receiving a thorough shaking up and painful bruises.

Shortly after the Bullhead arrived in Australia, Griff was transferred to Admiral Lockwood's operations staff at Guam. His replacement was Lieut. Comdr. Edward R. Holt, Jr., USN, a capable and experienced submariner who had made 10 war patrols in junior positions on the Grouper, Baya, and Sealion. Also relieved at the same time were "Eric" Erickson, Pat Doherty and nearly a score of enlisted men.

Holt was better known to his Navy comrades as "Skillet," a nickname given him years ago by an imaginative high school football coach. His new assignment marked the consummation of a burning desire to have command of a submarine before his 30th birthday on July 6. His orders to the Bullhead arrived July 4.

To his wife in South Carolina, Skillet wrote a long letter, the first page of which was an elaborate picture he had drawn of a huge exploding firecracker and his new address printed in red letters. Then followed pages of praise for the boat and crew, and his determination to "live up to the wonderful job Comdr. Griffith had done."

One line in particular described the new skipper's

complete joy over his promotion: "I couldn't have been more fortunate if I had written my own ticket."

A gala ship's party held in a gaudy, noisy Perth cabaret climaxed the fortnight of fun and frolic in Australia. Dinner-dancing was the main scheduled event, but the highlights of the gathering were an informal farewell speech by Comdr. Griffith, and a spectacular vocal duet by him and the lowest rated man on the sub, Hubert B. Hackett, steward's mate 2nd class, from Jamaica, N. Y. Accompanied by the Australian orchestra, they harmonized "Paper Doll," following the original arrangement. Then they broke into a snappy swing version that confounded the Aussies and forced them to drop out while the captain and Hackett finished minus the accompaniment.

This party, Brantley pointed out, was marked by the congeniality of the participants and the absence of fights. There wasn't even a scuffle, which was a trait of personality with the Bullhead men; they refused to fight among themselves, but God help an outsider who rated their notice.

A few days later, Comdr. Griffith conferred with his successor and suggested it might be a good idea to shell the small town of Ampenan on Lombok Island, while en route to the Java Sea. (During the refit, the Bullhead's forward 20-millimeter gun was replaced with another 40 and a second five incher was added forward.) Holt agreed and they discussed ways and means of carrying out the attack. He also planned to fire torpedoes at certain dock installations in an effort to destroy them.

Griff wound up his affairs at the Submarine Base while the Bullhead went to sea for additional training. On the morning he departed Perth for Guam, a messenger caught him at the airfield and delivered this dispatch sent on the regular submarine circuit through official channels:

OVERDUE AND PRESUMED LOST

Bullhead one on July twenty three
Sent to Griffith from us at sea.
While we are training for another punch
You are heading for the Guam home front.
'Take her down' is on our sched,
While yours calls for an armchair spread.
We wish you luck on every day
May paper dollies line your way.
We toast you proudly at the bar
Your crew we were, your friends we are.

Something began to twist and tear inside Griff. His eyes filled and nearly overflowed. He swallowed a couple of times, blew his nose noisily like a trumpet, and climbed aboard the big transport plane for the Marianas.

That was the last radio message ever transmitted by the Bullhead.

On the morning of July 31, 1945, a group of Comdr. Holt's close friends, including Lieut. Comdr. W. R. DeLoach, came aboard the submarine to wish him good luck. Holt had DeLoach send a cable to his wife, as he always did before leaving on patrol. A Navy chaplain conducted a short service — a prayer, the 23rd Psalm, a brief talk, and the hymn Rock of Ages. At one p.m., the Bullhead, her conning tower emblazoned with a huge colorful Bullhead insignia painted by her new skipper, sailed to join a wolf pack and carry out unrestricted warfare in the Java Sea.

The following day, Comdr. Holt met an incoming Allied vessel and planned to transfer mail. But the rough seas prevented the other craft from coming close enough and the Bullhead resumed her journey.

On August 2, Holt wrote that he felt as if they were in port as they were still eating fresh vegetables and fruit. Two days later, about 350 miles south of Lombok Strait, the Bullhead met the Dutch submarine 0-21, commanded by Lieut. F. J. Kroesen, RNN, heading south to Fremantle, and transferred a sack of mail for the States.

The Bullhead was neither seen nor heard from thereafter.

The first devastating atomic bomb was dropped on sprawling Hiroshima on August 6; three days later a second A-bomb was detonated over Nagasaki. A frantic, defeated Japanese government hurriedly sent out peace feelers. Everyone knew the end of a great war, a futile war, was in sight.

On August 13, two days before the official surrender announcement by Hirohito, dispatches were sent to all submarines in the Pacific, ordering them to "cease fire" and return to specific bases. The Bullhead was instructed to acknowledge receipt of the dispatch and proceed to Subic Bay.

Every submarine at sea, except the Bullhead, acknowledged her message. Staff officers thought her radio gear might have been temporarily disabled and had the "return home" order repeated for several days. They waited apprehensively, and when the fleet submarine failed to show up by August 23, the Navy Department immediately released Communique No. 623 at Guam and Washington:

1. The Submarine USS Bullhead is overdue from patrol and presumed lost. The Bullhead left Fremantle, Australia, on July 31, 1945 for operations in the Java Sea. Efforts to contact the Bullhead by radio began August 13 and have been unsuccessful. It is assumed that the Bullhead has been lost due to enemy action.

2. Next of kin of personnel on board have been notified.

The Navy broke precedent by this immediate announcement so that all ships could be publicly accounted for.

At the same time this news was published and broadcast throughout the country, wives and parents of men on the Bullhead were receiving letters dated up to August 4 which had been brought to Australia by the Dutch submarine then flown to the States. They were like messages from the great beyond.

Comdr. Griffith heard the news in a Navy hospital on Guam, where he was recuperating from general exhaustion. He could hardly believe the reports.

In a letter to me several days later he wrote:

"How hard it is for me to contemplate the end of that fine ship and her finer crew. Of course, she having been my ship, I am naturally prejudiced; but my opinion of the fine job turned in by officers and men was confirmed by every Squadron and Division Commander under whom we served. I am filled with compassion for the families of the men and have written to the wives whose addresses I could get. But I know how futile words must be to alleviate their sorrow.

"I believe the Bullhead was able to bombard Ampenan on Lombok. From my knowledge of the areas and their probabilities, I feel that the boat was possibly the victim of a Jap airplane as she was diving to escape. You know from experience how close they can get to a submarine before she gets under. A little more luck on the part of the plane is all that it takes. Comdr. Holt was thoroughly seasoned and nobody can consider the loss his fault. It could have happened to you and me."

In some sections of the United States it was the custom for the local minister to deliver casualty messages to families. When the telegram of notification arrived in Mrs. Holt's town, Laurens, S. C., her minister was absent and the Baptist preacher, Rev. J. H. Kizer, brought her the telegram. It did not mention the name of the submarine.

He told Mrs. Holt of his nephew, who had been in submarines throughout the war, and was lucky to come through without a scratch. When the minister returned to his home, he found a letter with the news that his nephew, William Mack Smith, of Bogue Chitto, Miss., was also missing — on the Bullhead.

A few days later, hopes of the next of kin zoomed when the New York Herald Tribune published the names of four Bullhead men as liberated from a Japanese prison camp. But the report proved to be erroneous; the names should have been listed in the "missing" column. And again the hearts of four score families hung heavy with anguish.

Many months later, a ragged envelope forwarded half-way around the world, from the fleet post office in Australia to Guam to Washington, finally caught up with Comdr. Griffith in Newport, R. I., where he was instructing at the Navy's General Line School.

It was a letter from the Michael Fina Company in New York, announcing they had a gift for him purchased by the officers and men of the Bullhead and would forward it as soon as they received a permanent mail address.

On August 6, 1946, exactly one year after the date the Bullhead was thought to be lost in North Lombok Strait, the package arrived, a poignant reminder from the past. The gift was a silver utility plate inscribed:

To Comdr. Walter T. Griffith, USN, from the officers and men who proudly served under him on the U.S.S. Bullhead.

Finis was written to the story of the Bullhead when the Secretary of the Navy, James Forrestal, wrote next of kin in late August 1946, that records indicated their son's death had occurred August 23, 1945; this having been established as the date the Bullhead was overdue at Subic Bay. (It does not indicate the date she was actually lost.)

* * * * *

DEDICATED TO THESE MEN ON THE BULLHEAD

OFFICERS

Lt. Comdr. Edward R. Holt, Jr.
Commanding Officer

Lt. Keith R. Phillips
Lt. Earl D. Hackman, Jr.
Lt. (jg) Paul A. Gossett
Lt. (jg) Donald O. Henriksen

Lt. (jg) Raymond W. Strassle
Lt. (jg) Joseph J. Parpal
Lt. (jg) Jack Simms II
Ens. Waldemar A. Kulczycki

ENLISTED MEN

Alfred Aiple, Jr., QM2c
Harold A. Anderson, Y2c
Robert H. Barringer, S1c
George L. Bell, MoMM1c
James D. Benner, S1c
Walter E. Bertram, MoMM2c
Harold R. Bridgstock, RT2c
Ralph M. Brume, MoMM2c
Kadzmir J. Buczek, TM2c
Richard B. Burns, CTM
Ray W. Church, MoMM1c
James F. Collins, EM3c
Howard E. Crandall, MoMM3c
Elmer M. Dahl, MoMM3c
Glen M. Davidson, F1c
Jerry K. Davidson, MoMM2c
Charles J. Day, EM2c
Charles W. Dougherty, SC1c
Edward M. Engebretsen, CQM
James R. Fahey, RM3c
Ralph G. Foster, F1c
Kenneth E. Foust, QM3c
Fred C. Fritz, RM2c
Charles W. Gay, EM3c
Joseph P. Gilheany, Jr., RM3c
Clyde M. Graves, S1c
William F. Greaves, EM3c
Hubert B. Hackett, StM2c
John L. Hancock, GM2c
John Junior Harris, QM3c
William P. Hawkins, EM2c
George V. Heaton, MoMM2c
Thomas P. Helferich, MoMM2c
LaVerne W. Huisman, S1c
William Ireland, TM2c
Lester L. Jenkins, EM2c
James R. Jensen, EM3c

Fred J. Jewell, QM2c
Percy Johnson, Jr., StM1c
Joseph W. Jones, CEM
Richard A. Keister, RT3c
Jacob J. Kopf, EM3c
Oscar V. Mannas, TM2c
Roy K. Marin, MoMM2c
Jack P. Markham, TM3c
Harry A. McDermott, MoMM3c
George P. Morgan, TM3c
Paul W. Olson, S1c
Paul F. Overbeek, S1c
Richard W. Palmer, F1c
William J. Parks, GM1c
Robert M. Pattengale, TM3c
Robert S. Patterson, SoM2c
William M. Peart, EM1c
Robert J. Perry, MoMM1c
Carl W. Piatt, SC3c
Richard A. Pinder, CMoMM
William J. Ralston, Jr., TM3c
Robert J. Ritchie, EM3c
John A. Roberts, EM1c
Jesse Sandoval, S1c
Lee A. Schlegel, F1c
Orville G. H. Schmidt, F1c
William E. Short, TM1c
Bert Shuey, Jr., SC3c
Dale M. Siefken, FCS2c
Edward Smida, PhM1c
Carl J. Smith, CRM
William M. Smith, CEM
Frank T. Stifter, RT2c
Charles H. Taylor, S1c
Melvin Tobias, MoMM3c
Andrew T. Watson, CMoMM
Lyle L. Webb, S1c

Elmer J. Wiersma, F1c

MESSAGE FROM SUBMARINE OVERDUE

by WIN BROOKS

We surfaced near dawn when the moon was thin
To charge the batteries, low as sin.
The sea was feathered; the breeze, which hung
Easterly, tickled along the tongue
Like dry champagne.   (Though I gravely fear
Sub crews are better acquainted with beer.)
The skipper stood with the O.O.D.
The deck watch added lookouts three,
And sparks, who is numbered among the drones,
Manned his phones.

The diesels gave us a steerage way
With light sea following.   So we lay
Bow for Formosa, stern to Wake,
Along the course that the Nip must make.
The night was going.   The Nip was coming,
There in the darkness faintly humming.
Varsity soundmen dialed his source,
First team plotters traced his course,
When suddenly up to the tight bridge deck
Climbed the Exec.

"Sir", he said in a voice indignant,
"Here is a message most malignant.
Pearl just coded an ALNAV through
That a submarine is overdue
And is, in the run of hard coin tossed,
Heads or tails, presumed to be lost."
He swore with admirably little fuss,
"The fools mean us!"

OVERDUE AND PRESUMED LOST

(We remember the depth charge blow,
But that was a long, long time ago.)
The skipper snorted a laugh of scorn.
"What in the sea green hell goes on?
We're a year from port with our oil tanks brimmed,
An enemy convoy all but limned,
Water condition A, tubes loaded —
Listed for obsequies outmoded!"
He scanned the night with a hungry frown.
"Take her down!"

The lights flashed green on the Christmas Tree,
We took her down to periscope—see.
Verbs and adjectives most inept,
We plotted course that would intercept.
Sea on scope made a hollow drumming
Heading her in. The dawn was coming.
The Jap was coming. The skipper's gaze
Fixed on the lead ships through the haze.
"Two is the target. Let one pass.
Heavy cruiser. Kako class.
Range three thousand, scale one hundred,
Bearing zero, zero three. I've one dread
Firing at dawn—that the fish we swim
Reflect on the red sun's rising rim,
And not the rim of the Rising Sun. . . .Fire One!"

We lurched as she left, remotely hissing.
(God guard our submarines from missing.)
We heeled and steadied; and at the eye
The skipper said, "Cargo. Pass her by. . . .
Troopship. Taigei class maru. . . .Fire Two!"

We waited taut while the stop watch ran,
We waited cold while the sweat began,
Till dull on the hull boomed distant thunder,
Crashing the new born day asunder.

OVERDUE AND PRESUMED LOST

"What do you make of One in the view, Sir?"
"Scratch the cruiser!"
Once repeated, we felt her shudder,
Shake like a dog from bow to rudder.
"What do you score for Two in the smother?"
"Scratch the other!"

Now take her down. . . .
             take her down. . . .
                         take her easily,
Slide her down. . .glide her
                   down silently, greasily,

Down where the bottom is,
Oh, fair the bottom is!
Our lair the bottom is,
Safe from attack.

Down. . .take her down
             . . .take her down
                        . . .take her down.

Now lay her gently and gently to sleep,
One
  mile
    deep!

(How can it ever be said we are lost
Who are always together?
Rime on our tomb from the deep's firefrost,
Always together, in battle and weather.
In death? Lost? Lost but breath.
We are gay, we are young, we are one, and one only.
One with the deathless and one with the living,
One in close comradeship, now never lonely,
But never forgiving
The silly assumption so carelessly tossed,
The stupid presumption: "Presumed to be lost.")

OVERDUE AND PRESUMED LOST

With radio silence C imposed,
How can we tell you we only dozed
There in the sand, in the mud, in the dark,
All hands secure, with an unquenched spark
Glowing to light the buoyant spirit
And blow the tanks?   Do you still not hear it?
How can we tell you there on land
What only the sub crews understand?
How can we say what the spirit means?
There is no death for submarines.

And nights when the moon hangs thin and low
From Truk to Guam to Hokkaido,
Submarines lying secure and deep
Presumed to be lost but only asleep,
Shudder and tremble and upward glide
A mile and more in the surging tide;
Shadows moving with never a wake
Along the course that the Nip must make—
Men of the vast, unsounded waters
At general quarters.

OVERDUE AND PRESUMED LOST
TICKET TO ADVENTURE

UNITED STATES PACIFIC FLEET
AND PACIFIC OCEAN AREAS
HEADQUARTERS OF THE COMMANDER IN CHIEF

A2-14

Serial 5670   19 Mar 1945

From: Commander in Chief, U.S. Pacific Fleet and
           Pacific Ocean Areas.

To: Mr. Martin SHERIDAN,
           Boston Globe.

Subject: Travel Authority.

1. Upon receipt of this letter, you are authorized to proceed to the port in which the U.S.S. BULLHEAD may be and upon arrival report to the Commanding Officer, U.S.S. BULLHEAD, for the purpose of gathering news material.

Copy to:
  ComSubPac
  ComFwdAreaCenPac
  ComSubPacAd
  CO, USS BULLHEAD

                              R. E. KEETON
                              By direction

....

FIRST ENDORSEMENT
SS332/P16-4/JJIB

                    U.S.S. BULLHEAD (SS332)
                    Care Fleet Post Office
                    San Francisco, California
                    21 March 1945

From: The Commanding Officer.

To: Mr. Martin SHERIDAN, Boston Globe.

1.   Reported this date.

                              W. T. GRIFFITH.

OVERDUE AND PRESUMED LOST

SUBMARINE SQUADRON TEN
CARE OF FLEET POST OFFICE
New York, New York

MY DEAR

In a letter recently received by me from Commander W. T. Griffith, U.S.N., the former Commanding Officer of the U.S.S. Bullhead, he asked that I convey the following message to you.

"While the loss of the Bullhead cannot have been as much of a shock to me as I know it was to you, I want you to know that were it possible for me to replace your loved one and send him back to you I would gladly do it.

"It would indeed be futile for me to offer you any hope, but for what consolation it may give I shall tell you all that I know.

"In the Bullhead we had the finest officers and men who ever sailed a Navy ship. Their united efforts and each individual's character and personality contributed materially to our success.

"On our first patrol we operated off Formosa and Hong Kong during the Okinawa invasion. While we found no enemy shipping we did get bombed a few times and bombarded a Jap Island on two occasions. About mid-patrol we picked up three badly wounded Army aviators near the China coast inside the minefields. For this deed the Admiral designated the patrol as a successful one. (Requirements for successful patrol are to sink at least one ship or to perform some other mission of comparable importance.) That is the significance of the little silver submarine; called the Submarine Combat Insignia. This patrol was also awarded a Battle Star to be worn by the men on the Asiatic-Pacific Area Campaign Ribbon for the Okinawa Operation.

"After the first patrol we refitted the ship in the Philippine Islands.

"On the second patrol we found some shipping in the Java Sea Area and succeeded in sinking four of them and damaging three in addition to acting in support of the Brunei Bay and Balikpapan landing.

"Off Batavia, we surfaced on a small convoy, chased off the two escorting picket boats, sank the largest vessel and chased a damaged ship into a harbor, where we finished shooting all our ammunition at ships at the docks.

"Of course our second patrol was 'successful' so that gave us a gold star on the silver submarine.

"When we got to Fremantle, West Australia, I was very

unhappy to find that I was being relieved of command and sent to a staff job; but they gave me no choice. The boys had a very nice stay in port and before I left I felt that they were quite satisfied with the new skipper — Lieutenant Commander Holt. Although this was his first command, he had made 10 previous war patrols and was very capable.

"The ship left Fremantle on July 31st to patrol again in the Java Sea. In the general vicinity there were several other submarines with whom they were to work, but none of those submarines ever contacted Bullhead by sight or radio. You may completely dismiss the idea that one of our own boats might have sunk them because we are all mutually cognizant of each vessel's general position, and we have special methods of recognizing and identifying each other even before we make sight contact.

"The ship was operating in waters near the islands, but if they had run aground they would have told us by radio before they destroyed the ship.

"I know the waters around the Java Sea very well, and it is my opinion that if the loss was due to enemy action it was by aircraft bombing. The only other possibility is that there was some failure in the operation of the ship; but knowing the ship and men so well, I personally discount this.

"In either of the above cases there is always the possibility that a few of them got ashore. Unofficially I have heard that a few survivors from at least six submarines were found in Japan, about whom we had previously had no word. If any of the boys got ashore they will be recovered by the British or Dutch occupation forces; but, as I said before, it would be an unkindness to attempt to offer you any hope. I can only say, and hope with you, that if this was the end for them that it was quick and clean, and that they went down fighting.

"Words are futile things at best so I shall say no more except to assure you that Mrs. Griffith and I are with you in your sorrow.

> Sincerely,
> W. T. GRIFFITH,
> Commander, U. S. Navy."

Since Commander Griffith was so well liked by the men who served with him, I feel certain that his letter will have a deep meaning to the loved ones left behind by these men.

> Sincerely,
> JAMES J. BRANTLEY
> Chief Yeoman, U. S. Navy.

OVERDUE AND PRESUMED LOST

UNITED STATES NAVY

The Commander Submarines, SEVENTH FLEET, has the honor to award the Submarine Combat Insignia and to commend in absentia

for services as set forth in the following

CITATION:

"The U.S.S. BULLHEAD on an offensive patrol in confined and heavily patrolled enemy waters North of Lombok Strait in the Java Sea failed to return as scheduled. There is no information regarding the number of successful attacks delivered against the enemy during this patrol but in view of the fine previous record of this ship, it is believed she was conducting bold and aggressive attacks up until the time she was declared missing.

As a member of the crew of the U.S.S. BULLHEAD, his exemplary devotion to duty contributed greatly to the success of this ship against the enemy. The Commander Submarines, SEVENTH FLEET, forwards this commendation in recognition of his splendid performance of duty, which is in keeping with the highest traditions of the Naval Service."

JAMES FIFE,

Rear Admiral, U. S. NAVY.

Another Bullhead decoration is the Battle Star for the Brunei Bay operation.

OVERDUE AND PRESUMED LOST

U.S. Naval School
General Line
Newport, R.I.
31 July 1946

From: Commander W. T. Griffith, USN

To   :   Next of Kin—U.S.S. BULLHEAD

On this anniversary of the last sailing of the BULLHEAD I have felt compelled to write you all again.

There is nothing new to say.

Our best information (including what could be gleaned after entering Japan) still is that the BULLHEAD was sunk by Japanese aircraft.

If there were any survivors I feel that they would have been found by now, as search teams have been sent into every part of the Pacific to look for them. If they were hit while in the process of diving there is little possibility that anyone got out.

In regard to the reports circulated among you (attributed third hand to Comdr. Peterson of Icefish) regarding BULLHEAD's last patrol, a copy was forwarded to me. As with all third hand information, this was quite garbled. Comdr. Peterson worked with BULLHEAD only on the second patrol—my last in command. We were ordered in to shallow water several times and succeeded in sinking four ships. Neither Icefish nor any other submarine was with BULLHEAD when she was lost.

We have reason to believe that BULLHEAD skillfully executed an attack which Comdr. Holt and I had planned together; but she was not lost as a result of this attack.

Martin Sheridan is back from Hollywood and is devoting this summer to completing the story of the BULLHEAD, and I am giving him what assistance I can.

Please let me know if there is any other information that I can give you.

May the peace of God be, and abide with you all.

W. T. GRIFFITH

GLOSSARY OF SUBMARINE TERMS

Boat ....Submarine (Although a submarine is technically a ship, submariners refer to her as a boat.)

Fish ....Torpedo

Sack ....Bunk

Hit the sack, hit the pad ....Go to bed

Sack artist ....Man who spends considerable time in his bunk.

Bulkhead ....Wall or partition

Hatch ....Door

Head ....Water Closet

Deck ....Floor

Wardroom ....Where officers mess (eat).

Spit kit ....Small enemy patrol boat — too small for a sub to torpedo, but large enough to carry depth charges.

Ashcan ....Depth charge

Zoomies, fly-fly boys ..Airplanes and pilots

Dive the boat ....Diving command used when sub is on surface.

Take her down ......Diving command used when boat is at periscope depth.

Up periscope ....Run up the periscope (sub's eyes when submerged.)

Down periscope ......Run down the periscope.

Ping jockey ....Soundman

Monkey wrench ......Motor machinist's mate

Bean jockey, stew burner or belly robber ..Cook

Old man ....Captain

Shaky Jake ....Chief electrician's mate

Flags or scivvy waver ..Signalman

Deck ape ....Deckhand

Snipe or bilge rat .....Fireman

Warhead or smooth bore ....Torpedoman

Doc, pill pusher or
   quack .... Pharmacist's mate
Gravity jockey .... Man in the electrical gang who checks
                          the gravity of the giant battery cells.
Transom .... Built-in leather covered seat in the ward-
                          room.
Riding the vents ..... Goldbricking (loafing)
Trailer .... After torpedo room
Bugs .... Chronometers (clocks)
Pressure happy .... Slap happy (dopey)
OD .... Officer of the deck
Scivvies .... Underpants
Take a fix .... Determine ship's position with sextant.
SNAFU .... Situation normal, all fouled up.
Scuttlebutt .... Rumors or drinking water fountain.
Trim dive .... Dive normally made at dawn every day
                          to check trim of sub — i.e., to correct
                          weights in the various compartments
                          and ballast tanks by compensating for
                          fuel burned and other changes so the
                          boat can dive instantly.
Pete .... Jap single engine float seaplane.
Sally, Betty .... Jap twin engine land based patrol
                          bombers.